Comments from those wh
Adulthood" Seminar

"Every Christian, in every Church needs to hear this message."
    (D.D.) Pastor in Denver, Colorado

"Best parenting seminar I've ever attended."
    (G.P.) Parent in Littleton, Colorado

"This seminar can change the youth of Brazil, every church in our country needs to hear this message"
    (J.N.) Ministry Leader in Brazil

"Some of the examples from Scripture you gave were incredible!
    (P.D.) Parent in Littleton, Colorado

"Your insight as a Jew is remarkable."
    (R.R.) Parent in Florida

"Every parent in Australia, no, in the world needs to hear this message"
    (G.W.) Pastor in Brisbane, Australia

"This must be God, as He appears to have hidden this simple yet so profound a revelation for such a time as this."
    (J.C.) Pastor in Dallas, Texas

"I've been a Christian for more than 20 years...been to hundreds of seminars....thought I heard it all... until today."
    (L.C.) Parent in Kansas City, Missouri

Stepping
Into
Adulthood

by
Jeff Brodsky

ACW Press
5501 N. 7th Ave. #502
Phoenix, AZ 85013

Cover design by Eric Walljasper
Page design by Steven R. Laube
Typeset using Electra 12pt. Designed in 1935 by William Addision Dwiggins, Electra has been a standard book typeface since its release because of its evenness of design and high legibility.

Unless otherwise noted, all Scripture verses are taken from the *Holy Bible,* New King James Version copyright © 1982 by Thomas Nelson Publishers. Used by permission.

Scripture quotations marked NIV are taken from the *Holy Bible*, New International Version, copyright © 1973, 1978, 1984 by International Bible Society. Used by permission of Zondervan Publishing House. All rights reserved.

Publisher's Cataloging-in-Publication
(Provided by Quality Books, Inc.)
Brodsky, Jeff.
    Stepping Into Adulthood / Jeff Brodsky -- 1st ed.
    p. cm.
    Includes bibliographical references
    ISBN 0-9656749-2-4

    1. Church Work With Teenagers. 2. Initiations rites--Religious aspects--Christianity. 3. Puberty rites. 4. Parent and teenager--Religious aspects--Christianity. 5. Adolescent psychology. I. Title.
BV4447.B76 1997   259'.23
                  QBI97-41164

Printed in the United States of America

To obtain more copies please contact:
Joy International
P.O. Box 5399
Littleton, CO 80155-5399
303-766-2650 Toll Free: 1-888-JOY-4-ALL
Website: http://www.joy.org
E-mail: jeff@joy.org

Contents

Dedication

As I thought of the many people who have influenced my life over the almost ten-year period as I wrote this book, there are only three people who continually come to my mind who have been there for me every day from the moment I began this book. It is to these three that I lovingly dedicate this book.

When my son Lance spoke the words, "Daddy, I want to be a man," to me in 1987, I realized for the first time in my life that I had an incredible responsibility of training and preparing him for manhood. How does one do that when they are not prepared themselves? Because of his sincere desire, I began the journey myself of understanding that responsibility and doing all that I could with what I knew to impart into my son's life what it meant to be a true man. When I saw that he was truly taking those first "steps into adulthood," I knew it was a time of celebration that I wanted to share with everyone I could. Those years of research became the basis for the "rite of passage" ceremony along with the Stepping Into Adulthood Seminars that I now conduct throughout the world. Lance has taught me many things about manhood as I watched him mature into the young man he is today. His love for the Lord, respect and honor to his mother and me, along with his devotion as a brother and friend to his sister, Jeni, has taught me so much over the years. It is through his life that much of what you read in this book was put into practice. The success of his "stepping into adulthood" has proven to me that the principles in this book really do work.

My daughter, Jeni, has matured into an awesome woman of God. I will never forget the special moment we shared as we walked together one clear, summer, moonlit night when she was only fifteen. She was preparing to leave the next morning for Florida, where she would train with Teen Missions to be a young missionary in the Australian Bush. As we spoke, I realized that I was releasing her into a new dimension in her life. As I look back on it, I now see that that mission trip was her moment of "stepping into adulthood." Little did I know that within the next few years she would travel and share our mutual love for children in Africa as well as other parts of the world. When I visited her in South Africa where she lived for a year while attending a Bible School, I had the privilege of seeing her minister to a roomful of excited, eager, enraptured Zulu children. For so many years, she had been the one who observed me. Now it was my turn to stand at the back of the room, as I proudly beheld that my little girl had surely become a beautiful young woman.

When Gail came into my life in 1974, I'm sure she had no idea what was in store for her in the coming years. In 1997 we celebrate twenty-three wonderful years together. How she has stayed with me all these years is a book and testimony in itself. I can't imagine it being easy staying married to a clown! The Purple Heart she received from a friend for living with me faithfully, is definitely deserved. Gail has been my strength throughout each of the years since that wonderful day in 1974 when we wed. There is no question in my mind that without her encouragement from the day this project began over ten years ago, you would not be reading this, because it never would have been completed. It is due to her encouraging me, motivating me, and inspiring me through these years that this book has finally come to print. Although the words have been penned by me, I give just as much of the credit for its completion to Gail. If any woman should ever receive the reward for both Woman of the Century, Mother of the Century, and Wife of the Century - I nominate Gail Brodsky.

As a result of the influence these three have had in my life, I dedicate this book to each of them. They have stuck with me every moment. Even during times (and there were many) of frustration, moodiness, and inner turmoil, they were there for me. They sacrificed many hours away from me as I sat at my computer until the wee hours of the morning writing. They recognized the importance and significance in the lives of each one who would read this book and put these words and principles into practice. Though there have been many who have been there for me over the years — only these three have been there every day since the day this book became a thought to me. Without each of them, this book never would have happened.

I lovingly dedicate this book to my wife, Gail, my daughter, Jeni, and my son, Lance. Finally!

Special Dedication

This special dedication is for my mom—Roz Brodsky. The Rock. Most women who have gone through what my mom has over the years would have given up a long time ago. If there is anyone on this earth for whom the phrase *"stick-to-it-tiveness"* applies, it's my mom. As a Jewish believer who has had the opportunity to speak all over the world, many have heard me talk about my *"Yiddisha Mama."* I have begun each of my talks with the words, *"I'm what's known as a Jewish mother's nightmare. Jewish mothers do not raise their sons to become Christian ministers."* Although I was a nightmare throughout my teenage years, my mother never stopped loving me. In my many years in the ministry, I have spoken to a myriad of people from all walks of life. I have heard some of the worst horror stories of what people have gone through. Many of them just up and quit. Yet through all the trials and tribulations in her life, she persevered with a fortitude and determination I have rarely seen in others. She truly is a Rock. When I first accepted Yeshua (the Hebrew for Jesus), with all my heart I wanted my family, (especially my mom) to understand that I was not giving up my Judaism—but that my Judaism was being completed in Him. I longed for the day that we would (together) proclaim Yeshua as Messiah. I received Yeshua (Jesus) in 1976, and that day has yet to come for my mom, but I'm confident it will, thanks to the prayers of literally thousands who are daily bringing the name "Roz" before the throne of God.

Mom, I will always treasure your wisdom, courage, and strength.

I give this special dedication to my mom—Roz Brodsky. *"I only want to see you there, Mom."*

Acknowledgements

Over the last ten years, there are many people who have touched and affected my life. Each of the following people has had a special impact on my life in a way that influenced some part of this book. I am grateful in knowing each one of them.

My incredible editor Steve Laube from ACW Press— other than my family, Steve stuck with me for ten years. I could not have completed this book without his encouragement and editorial expertise. It's a long time since that lunch, Steve! My "spiritual mama" Ann Noel—it's about time, Ann! Dave and Bonnie Duell of Faith Ministries COC—they taught me faith and gave me freedom. Mike and Marilyn Phillipps of Marriage Ministries International, Craig Hill of Family Foundations International—they gave me hours of counsel and wise advice. Incredible friends and encouragers: Eric and Lisa Traylor; Pat and Robin Davis, Mark and Lynnie Roche; Chuck Eaton; Ed Yacknin and Lynn Myers. All the following pastors: Ed Delph of Hosanna Christian Fellowship in Arizona; Bruce and Claudia Porter of Celebration Christian Church; Mark and Susi Miller; The Geist Family (thanks for the cabin and the peace and quiet); Peter and Rebecca Laue (God's Stretcher Bearers allowed me to heal when I was hurting); and Ed and Mary Mast. Ed not only took the time to tell me of the Messiah, but he faithfully discipled me in those early years when I was voracious in wanting to know more. I'm still hungry after all these years, Ed. A special thank you to my proofreaders Sandee Dybdahl and Linda Busk.

Max Lucado for speaking these words to me:

"Jeff, a book like this will continue to give, even after you're gone."

Finally, where would I be without my Messiah, Yeshua ha' Mashiach—Jesus, my Savior and my Lord? Without Him I am nothing. It is to Him that I give all the glory and honor.

INTRODUCTION

I was invited to speak as a "guest rabbi" at the Bar Mitzvah ceremony and celebration of Jesse Porter. I knew Jesse fairly well, since he was a part of my youth group, as well as one of only two youths (his sister, Naomi, being the other) who, along with my son, had gone on four 101-mile walks across Death Valley with me. You really get to know a person when you spend that much time with them walking for several hours a day in the quietness and beauty of the desert. It wasn't until after the ceremony, at the celebration, that I understood what the past several years of research and study had helped me achieve. The realization came when Rich, one of the guests, came to me and said, "Wow, I didn't know there was an expert in this field."

"Excuse me?" I said.

He continued by saying, "Jeff, you were the rope today. What you said really tied everything together in a way that helped people to understand everything that was going on here. I didn't really know what we were here for, until you shared the significance and purpose of our supporting Jesse in his 'passage into manhood.' Thanks a lot. I really appreciate you."

Whew! I never realized that the past nine and a half years meant so much. But I do know that without the diligent hours of research and study I would not be able to speak around the world on the subject of the "rite of passage."

It is a real blessing to see the response of Christians when they fully understand the principles set forth through having this type of service. In so doing, they come to recognize its validity and significance in the lives of their children.

For the last ten years I have studied, researched, and spent literally thousands of hours talking with parents, youth workers, pastors, youth, and children across America. I spoke with them in their cities, in their churches, at conventions, conferences, seminars, over the Internet, wherever I could find someone who would talk on the subject. When I traveled around the world, I would engage in conversation with anyone I could find from Australia to Europe to the Middle East to Asia and even the Maasai tribesmen in Africa. I listened to anyone who could tell me what they knew, and if and how they practiced any form of a "rite of passage." I was voracious in my desire to know more about this all too neglected yet vital area.

Now that the book is in your hands, it is my deepest desire to see the information found within these pages, be used to give you a greater understanding of the needs of your own children. The easiest way to take a journey is to have a guide. God gave children parents to be the guides in their lives. May God bless your efforts as you guide your children on their journey - from being your child, to Stepping Into Adulthood that will help them become the man or woman of God that He created them to be.

PART ONE

A FAMILY JOURNEY

CHAPTER ONE

WHAT'S A NICE JEWISH BOY LIKE ME DOING IN A CHURCH LIKE THIS?

As a prelude to our exploration of the "rite of passage" let me give you a bit of my journey to help you understand why this is such an important subject.

I'm what's known as a Jewish mother's nightmare. Let me explain. Jewish mamas do not raise their little boys to grow up to become Christian ministers! When little Jeffrey (that's me) was born, I'm sure my mama didn't look at my dad and say, "*Look honey, it's a boy! Wouldn't it be wonderful if he grew up to be a Christian minister and is used by God to tell people all over the world about Jesus?!*" I don't think so. Actually, the first time I tried to tell my family about my new found faith in Yeshua was disastrous. In my exuberance and zeal, along with a yearning for them to receive Yeshua as their Messiah, I got upset when my family questioned what I did. Little did I realize that in Orthodox Jewish homes, the family would actually have a complete funeral service for the one who had accepted Yeshua as their Messiah. Fortunately for me, my family was of the ultra liberal Jews in New York.

It was this liberal attitude toward my Judaism that caused me to denounce my faith in Judaism and all belief in God years later. I was brought up with so much confusion and so many questions about what a Jew actually was. This confusion began when I was a little boy growing up on the streets of New York. Our neighborhood in the East Flatbush section of Brooklyn was made up of mostly Jews. All my friends were Jews. Most of their families were just like mine, ultra liberal in their faith.

Oh, we were Jews all right. When the time was right. On the high holy days, we had to cover all the mirrors in our house. We kept the TV turned off. We wouldn't eat if we were over thirteen. We couldn't carry any money outside, and we couldn't drive our car.

When no one was around to observe our adherence to the rules, though, I saw a different story. The people in my home as well as my friends' homes all looked in the mirror, then covered them up before going out. The TVs were left on until someone knocked on the door. Everybody had something to eat. I know that most adults carried money. And I saw lots of the people from the synagogue park their cars around the corner, then walk to the temple.

What's the deal? I thought. If these were "holy" days, why wasn't God doing something dramatic to these people?

Everything changed when I walked into the temple. I don't know if others noticed it, but there was a certain reverence there. It was where I first remember seeing people talking to God. It was the only place I actually saw any form of praise or worship. With the little knowledge and understanding an eleven-year-old boy could have, I came to the conclusion that the only place God really saw you was when you were in the temple.

I was in the temple so infrequently after the age of thirteen that sin became commonplace for me. If I felt the need for forgiveness, I could always go to the temple one day a year on Yom Kippur (the day of atonement for the Jews), say a series of prayers, and come out feeling free. At least until the first cigarette, pipeful of marijuana or hashish, or some off-color remark and joke about the opposite sex.

I soon abandoned all belief in the God of Abraham and all other religions. I found faith of any kind meaningless and a complete waste of time.

It was after the death of my older brother Steven, who was eighteen, that I finally came to believe there was no

God. I was only sixteen at the time when my brother died of cancer. He suffered excruciating pain at the end, and I refused to accept the fact that a God who calls us His "Chosen People" would cause one of those chosen ones to suffer the way Steven did. It just wasn't fair. My brother had everything to live for. I had nothing to live for. If God needed to take someone, why wasn't it me? I was involved with drugs, illicit sex, and I had dropped out of high school. I was of no use to anybody. My brother had a special talent with cars. He could take a car apart and put it back together. He had great friends. He was engaged to a beautiful girl who stayed by his side until the end. He had everything to live for, where as I had made a shambles of my life. It wasn't until many years later that I learned that in reality it wasn't that I didn't believe in God. I was just so mad at Him for what I thought He did to my brother, and the pain and suffering that my family experienced.

After my brother's death, I realized that my life could be snatched from me at any time, so I decided to live it up while I could. For the next two years I had as much fun as possible. Then I joined the United States Air Force, where they tried to make a man out of me. I was stubborn and determined to get as much fun out of life as I could. When I got out of the Air Force, I wandered around from job to job for a few years. I met my wife Gail in March of '74 at the age of twenty-one. We were married eight months later. Nobody thought it would last. My parents. Her parents. My friends. Her friends. They all said it would end in six months. Now we are approaching our twenty-fifth anniversary. We're more in love now than when we first met, and our relationship keeps getting better and better.

In actuality, they were pretty right on. Our relationship would not have lasted more than a couple of years if one thing had not occurred. We both received Jesus as our Messiah and Lord during our third year of marriage.

After we were married, we decided it would be best to bring up our children in a completely different environment. At that time Gail and I had an opportunity to travel to Fountain Hills, Arizona, on a free trip. We fell in love with the area. Fountain Hills was so totally different than anything I had ever seen before. It was a dream come true. We bought a home and moved as soon as we could.

I had never been confronted by Christians before. The first Christian I remember meeting was when I was ten years old. Her name was Clara. She was Catholic, and all I remember was that during the Christmas season we would go over to her house and look at her tree. When I was fourteen, we moved to an area of Brooklyn called Canarsie. Our street was filled with Italians. Many of my friends at that time were Italian. They, too, were Catholic, and had Christmas trees. I was pretty close with some of these guys and their religion was no better than mine. We all sinned together pretty regularly.

When I was first confronted by a Christian I was taken aback. These people were nothing like what I ever saw or met before.

In Fountain Hills, I became very involved with the community. I had started my own business and was well respected for a twenty-four-year-old. I was really involved with the local school where my son Brent was in the first grade. I remember a Parent-Teacher meeting where the people were discussing which minister they were going to invite to pray before a special event the school was having. I was enraged. I pounded my fist on the desk and shouted, "No way! That's against the law. If you bring anybody in this school to pray, you better bring the one they're praying to, or I'll sue this school for every penny I can get!" Silence filled the room. The discussion was over. They knew I was right. It was the law. At the end of the meeting a woman came over to me. She was the first real Christian who ever spoke to me. I'll never forget her words: "I've never met anyone like you before. I'm going to pray for you every day until God reveals himself to you." I retorted with, "Don't waste your time."

I didn't know this until after I had received Jesus as my Messiah, but that dear, precious, sweet sister went home and called every prayer chain she could find throughout the United States. God was literally bombarded with the name Jeff Brodsky. It was no more than a week later that I started to run into Christians everywhere! For the first twenty-five years of my life I had never seen a real Christian, now they were all over the place.

I remember the first time I met the man who eventually led me to the Lord. He was the pastor of a local church in Fountain Hills and the president of the local Kiwanis Club. I needed to see him regarding something I was upset about. When he gave me the address where to meet him, little did I know that it was at his church office. When I first arrived there, I thought, *No way. I'm not goin' in there. But then I thought, Why not? There's nothing to be afraid of. I don't believe in God anyway.*

When I walked into the foyer, I saw a typical picture of Jesus. Strange, how I never knew much about Him, but I knew it was Him represented on the canvas hanging on the wall. As I gazed at the picture, His eyes seemed to follow me as I walked by. It was unnerving. I even began walking backward to see if I was imagining it. But wherever I walked, the eyes would follow. I figured it must have been an optical illusion. The chills I got up and down my spine as I closed the door of the sanctuary and left the eyes of Jesus behind me were real, though.

As I walked into the sanctuary, I was overtaken by a sense that I had only felt years earlier when I entered the synagogue. I knew deep within that this was a place that people believed was God's House. I knocked on the door of the pastor's office.

When I first met Pastor Ed Mast of the United Brethren Church, I was ready to do battle. There was something going on in the community with the Kiwanis Club that I disagreed with strongly, and I had no qualms about letting my feelings be made known. However, the battle never came. It's very difficult to fight with someone who is full of love. He overcame me with his genuineness and we ironed out our differences rather quickly.

As I was walking to the door with Pastor Ed, we were approached by his secretary. After the introductions, she came right out and asked me where I attended church. When I informed her I didn't, she asked why? I told her I didn't believe in God, the church, or anything to do with religion. She then became the second person in my life who made the statement to me, *"I'm going to pray for you."* I said, "That's nice. So is someone else. But I think you're wasting your time." I looked at Pastor Ed and saw a grin that simply showed a calm assurance. I got the feeling that he knew something I didn't know yet.

It was just a few days after that meeting that I began running into Christians wherever I went. If I went to a restaurant, all of a sudden I would notice people (and hear them) right next to me as they prayed over their meals. I couldn't remember a single time in my life seeing that happen. Now it happened almost daily.

I remember the moment it happened. As I look back, I can imagine this scenario in heaven. I can picture our heavenly Father sitting there with Jesus at His right hand. All of a sudden, He's bombarded with prayers for a nice Jewish boy from Brooklyn.

"Who's Jeff Brodsky?" He asks His Son.

"I don't know, I've never met him," replies Jesus.

"Let's check him out, there's people praying for him all over the place."

As they look at my life, they see something (and Some-one) missing, and I can imagine God saying, "We've got to do something about this guy. Holy Spirit, get him!"

I was driving on the Beeline Highway in Arizona at the time. I remember the sun shining on a nice hot September morning, when all of a sudden a presence entered my car. I don't know how to describe it, other than to say that I believe with all my heart that God sent an angel or some form of His presence into my vehicle. It was so strong that I literally had to stop driving. I pulled the car over and checked it from top to bottom. I looked in the trunk, under the seats, under the hood. There was unquestionably some kind of presence in my car that sent a chill up and down my spine. From that moment to this day that presence has never left me. As a matter of fact, it has continually grown stronger as I've built my relationship with God.

It was as if God reached into the car that morning and placed something inside me. I became obsessed with wanting to know more about God. Questions flooded my mind. Questions I had no answers to. But I knew someone who did. Within a few days, I called Pastor Ed. I decided that if anyone could answer my questions, he could. I had a respect for him that I never had for any other man before. Maybe it was be-cause I had never really met a man who had devoted his life so completely to God as he had. He seemed to be someone I could actually speak to on this level and share the questions that burned within me.

I invited him to my home and was astounded at the wis-dom he had in answering all my questions. It wasn't enough. I was insatiable. The hunger God had placed deep within me continued to grow. The more I learned the more I wanted to know. "What about Jesus?" Where did He fit in all of this? I needed to know more about Him. Was He really the prom-ised Messiah? If so, why did the Jews reject Him?

Pastor Ed left me with a paperback Bible. I couldn't accept it as the Word of God because it didn't look like it to me. I remember as a child, when we were in the temple, if anyone ever dropped their Bibles, they would immediately pick it up, dust it off, and look to the heavens as they kissed their Bibles in apology for dropping the Word of God. I had been ingrained with a reverence for the Word that stuck with me even as I grew and denied any belief in the One who gave us that Word. In paperback form, it simply did not have the same effect.

All during this time, I was attending a Real Estate school in Scottsdale, Arizona. Little did I know that God had already begun answering the prayers that were being spoken on my behalf. One afternoon during a break, I was approached by Jude Mandel, a real estate broker from Tempe, Arizona. After introducing himself he said, "I like the way you handle yourself when you speak. I'd like to take you to lunch and talk to you about coming to work for me." When I agreed, we went out to his car. It was a brand-new Corvette. It didn't take much to impress me in those days, and I was impressed. The next day he invited me to lunch again. This time we got into his second car, a brand-new Lincoln. I was hooked. Over the years I learned that if you wanted to be successful, you had to learn from one who already was a success.

When I finished the course and passed the real estate exam, I went to work for Mandel and Associates. Fortunately, at the time I did not know that Jude's younger brother Jan was a Christian. I knew I was going to share an office with him, but what I didn't know was that this twenty-two-year-old young man was Peter and Paul rolled into one. If I had known that, I never would have agreed to share that office. To this day, I thank God for sending Jan into my life. He was a virtual witnessing machine. So much so, that it came to the point of a confrontation between us. I would come home at night and tell my wife that if this guy didn't stop talking about Jesus, I would break his neck.

I met with Pastor Ed again, and he asked me to come to a service one Sunday. When I agreed, I was shocked. *How can I go to a church service?* I thought. When Sunday morning came, I decided there was no way I was going to walk into a Christian church service. Yes, I wanted to know more. And even though I had no qualms about boldly stating I was an atheist, I knew deep within that I was still a Jew. Nothing would ever stop me from being one. The more Christians would witness to me, the stronger my pride grew for my Jewish heritage. That pride grew out of the love these Christians showed me, and the sincere joy that filled their faces when I would tell them I was a Jew. Through the encouraging words of Christians, I began to fully understand what being one of God's chosen people as a Jew was all about. I never really understood my Judaism until it was shown to me by those who had a deep respect for His people in a way I had never experienced before. All I knew about being a Jew was what I had learned as a child. Growing up, there was always a lack of trust for others concerning my Judaism. Early on I quickly learned that people from other religions were out to "get" the Jews. The cry from Jews all over the world regarding the Holocaust was always "Never again!" I always wondered, "What if?"

But I had never been approached by real, genuine Christians. As a result, my pride for being a Jew began to rise up within me. I couldn't go to that Sunday morning service at a "church." So I called some friends early that morning and asked them if they wanted to go for a walk in the mountains with me. Three of us went that morning. While walking down a hill, something happened that changed my life forever. There was nothing in front of me as I walked down the hill. All of a sudden, it was as if something (or someone) tripped me. I remember falling and rolling down the hill. When I came to a stop, all I felt was an excruciating pain in my right foot. It hurt so bad that I could not stand up. The men who were with me had to carry me to the car. As they drove me to the emergency room, all I could think was, "If only I had gone to that church service this morning." I couldn't get the thought that God was "after me" out of my mind.

After the x-rays were taken, the doctor came in and told me the bad news. He informed me that what had happened was in between a fracture and a break. The pain was unbearable. After he treated me, I went home and continually had that same thought, "If only I had gone to that church service today."

The following Sunday I went on crutches. When I walked into the foyer, I stared at that same picture of Jesus, and His eyes seemed to follow me again as I entered the sanctuary. Chills went up and down my spine again. I sat in the back row in the chair closest to the exit. I was ready to leave as fast as I could if anything weird happened. As I sat there, it was as if only the pastor and I were in that room. I felt as if he could see inside me as he spoke words that pierced my heart. I left that morning with a feeling I've never had in my entire life. I began to sense a peace that I longed for, but it wasn't complete yet.

I went the following Sunday and learned they were showing a movie on Wednesday night. The title of the movie was *Time to Run*, a film produced by Billy Graham. During those three days, I was stuck at home. The pain in my foot was so great that I couldn't even drive my car. As I sat at home, I read several books that people had given to me about the Jewishness of Jesus. In my ignorance, I was amazed to discover that Jesus was actually a Jew. He lived His entire life as a Jew. As I studied, I came to the conclusion that if I was going to get as much information as to who the Messiah was, it was going to come from the Old Testament. I knew the New Testament would say everything I needed to hear about the Savior, but I needed to see who the Messiah was from what I knew as the Jewish Bible. As I read, I was amazed to learn of all the prophecies regarding who the coming Messiah would be. I was astounded when I saw that every Scripture reference as to who the Messiah would be was fulfilled in Jesus. Here are some of the ones that truly opened my eyes:

PROPHETIC SCRIPTURE FULFILLED

Prophecy

Fulfillment

Micah 5:2
But you, Bethlehem Ephrathah, Though you are little among the thousands of Judah, Yet out of you shall come forth to Me The One to be Ruler in Israel, Whose goings forth are from of old, From everlasting.

Luke 2:4,5,7
Joseph also went up from Galilee, out of the city of Nazareth, into Judea, to the city of David, which is called Bethlehem, because he was of the house and lineage of David, to be registered with Mary, his betrothed wife, who was with child...And she brought forth her first-born Son, and wrapped Him in swaddling cloths, and laid Him in a manger, because there was no room for them in the inn.

Isaiah 7:14
Therefore the Lord Himself will give you a sign: Behold, the virgin shall conceive and bear a Son, and shall call His name Immanuel.

Luke 1:26,27,30,31
Now in the sixth month the angel Gabriel was sent by God to a city of Galilee named Nazareth, to a virgin betrothed to a man whose name was Joseph, of the house of David. The virgin's name was Mary… Then the angel said to her, "Do not be afraid, Mary, for you have found favor with God. "And behold, you will conceive in your womb and bring forth a Son, and shall call His name Jesus.

Zechariah 9:9
Rejoice greatly, O daughter of Zion! Shout, O daughter of Jerusalem! Behold, your King is coming to you; He is just and having salvation, Lowly and riding on a donkey, A colt, the foal of a donkey.

Mark 11:7-9
Then they brought the colt to Jesus and threw their clothes on it, and He sat on it....Then those who went before and those who followed cried out, saying: "Hosanna! 'Blessed is He who comes in the name of the LORD!'"

Psalm 78:2-4
I will open my mouth in a parable; I will utter dark sayings of old, which we have heard and known, And our fathers have told us. We will not hide them from their children, telling to the generations

Matthew 13:34,35
All these things Jesus spoke to the multitude in parables; and without a parable He did not speak to them, that it might be fulfilled which was spoken by the prophet, saying: "I will open My mouth in parables; I will

to come the praises of the
LORD, and His strength and
His wonderful works that He
has done.

Isaiah 53:3
He is despised and rejected
by men, A Man of sorrows
and acquainted with grief.
And we hid, as it were, our
faces from Him; He was
despised, and we did not
esteem Him.

Psalm 34:20
He guards all his bones;
Not one of them is broken.

Psalm 41:9
Even my own familiar friend
in whom I trusted, Who ate
my bread, Has lifted up his
heel against me.

Isaiah 50:6
I gave My back to those who
struck Me, And My cheeks
to those who plucked out the
beard; I did not hide My face
from shame and spitting.

utter things kept secret
from the foundation of the
world."

John 1:11
He came to His own, and
His own did not receive
Him.

John 19:32,33
Then the soldiers came
and broke the legs of the
first and of the other who
was crucified with Him.
But when they came to
Jesus and saw that He was
already dead, they did not
break His legs.

Luke 22:48
But Jesus said to him,
"Judas, are you betraying
the Son of Man with a
kiss?"

Matthew 26:67
Then they spat in His face
and beat Him; and others
struck Him with the palms
of their hands.

Isaiah 53:12
Therefore I will divide Him a portion with the great, And He shall divide the spoil with the strong, Because He poured out His soul unto death, And He was numbered with the transgressors, And He bore the sin of many, And made intercession for the transgressors.

Mark 15:27,28
With Him they also crucified two robbers, one on His right and the other on His left. So the Scripture was fulfilled which says, "And He was numbered with the transgressors."

Psalm 22:17
I can count all My bones. They look and stare at Me.

Matthew 27:35
Then they crucified Him, and divided His garments, casting lots, that it might be fulfilled which was spoken by the prophet: "They divided My garments among them, And for My clothing they cast lots."

These are just ten examples of some three hundred prophecies relating to who the Messiah would be. Every one of them are fulfilled in Yeshua ha' Mashiach (the Hebrew for Jesus Christ). After intense study and deep searching for the truth, I had come to the conclusion that Jesus was who He claimed to be. There was absolutely no doubt in my mind.

That Wednesday evening, October 17, 1976, after the movie *Time To Run*, Pastor Ed stood before the congregation and gave an invitation to receive Jesus. It was as if the Holy Spirit Himself lifted me from my chair as I stood and accepted that invitation. I went with Pastor Ed into his office. We prayed and I left that office a new man. I've never been the same since.

When I left the church that night, the greatest desire I had was for a new Bible. A real one. The paperback that Pastor Ed gave me just didn't feel right to me. The next day I decided to drive to my office (about twenty miles from home). The pain in my foot was still so great that I had to drive with my left foot. When I arrived no one was there. When I walked into my office, I found a brand-new Bible sitting on my desk. A gift from my new brother in the Lord, Jan Mandel.

As a new Christian, I became voracious in my desire to grow and know everything about my newfound faith. I became so caught up with understanding my new life as a Christian that I put my Jewish faith behind me. It wasn't until ten years later, sitting in a synagogue in New Jersey while attending the Bar Mitzvah of my nephew, that my eight-year-old son Lance asked me a question, then made a statement that sent me on a ten-year search, resulting in this book.

Jesus said,
"And you shall know the truth,
and the truth shall make you free."
John 8:32

Chapter Two

WHOSE CHILD IS THIS?
THE MIRACLE OF LANCE

"Daddy, I want to be a man."

Those words (spoken by my then eight year old son Lance) rang deep within me over the next few years.

Those words would truly alter my life. He made this bold yet sincere statement to me after asking me this question; "Dad, am I gonna have a Bar-Mitvah?"

After asking him why, he simply stated, "Because Daddy, I want to be a man."

How can I give my son what he's asking for? I thought.

Traveling over 2,000 miles from Fountain Hills, Arizona, to New Jersey for my nephew Adams' Bar Mitzvah that year made an incredible impression on my son. But then Lance had always been special. Not to take anything away from my other children—Jeni and Brent—Lance was just different. He had to be different. I knew about him before he was born.

It took more than five years before I would share the story publicly, because I thought people would think I was out of my mind. After seeing the way people responded, though, I've told it all over the world.

It was a time of immense confusion for me. Here I was, this nice Jew from Brooklyn, New York, living in Fountain Hills, Arizona, working as a real estate salesman. I was making more money than I had ever dreamed of, and I had a wonderful wife, a super son, and a darling daughter. I just purchased a brand-new T-Bird with all the trimmings. I was purchasing a new home with a swimming pool. By the world's standards, I had it made! There was one thing about me that was different than most Jews I knew. I had received Jesus as my Messiah three years earlier. I was "born again." "A Jew for Jesus."

Jesus (or Yeshua, as many Jews prefer the Hebrew way of saying that wonderful name) had become everything to me. I yearned to serve Him, but I was too busy making plans to become a millionaire real estate mogul. My job made me money, but it made me miserable. Money had long lost its stronghold on me as a god. Yeshua was now my Lord and God! I was torn by what I believed my family wanted me to become — and by what my Lord wanted me to become. His servant.

It was a beautiful Arizona desert evening in April of 1978. Gail, Jeni, and Brent had already gone to bed. At this point in my life I truly needed answers from my heavenly Father. That evening my position for my prayer time took on a different form. Normally I would sit in a chair, or kneel with my head bowed as I prayed. Not that night. I lay face down, prostrate before God. As I lay flat on the ground in total submission before my Lord, I began to pour my heart out to Him. I wept uncontrollably as I poured out the anguish from deep within. I told Him about the confusion I felt and the heartache I had for not serving Him totally. I expressed the deep desire I had to share the love I had for His Son Yeshua in any way I could.

Have you ever noticed that when we pray, asking God to hear us and answer us, and finish our prayer "...in Jesus' name," we do the strangest thing? Without hesitation, we get up and leave. How can our Father speak to us when we don't give Him the time or opportunity to answer us? The Scriptures say "...be still, and know that I Am God."

He yearns to speak to us and answer our heart's cry. Yet we leave before we even give Him the chance to speak to us.

We have so many requests and questions, but we don't wait for His answers.

That night I cried out for answers. After praying, I lay there silently, waiting for the answers I so desperately needed. Suddenly, with no fanfare, no blaring trumpets, no harps playing in the background, I heard His voice as He spoke these words: "You're going to lose your job in a week; your wife is pregnant; you're going to have a son." My body tingled from head to toe as I heard those unusual words, yet all I could say was, "What?" Then God spoke those exact words to me again.

Whew! That was it. It wasn't exactly what I expected to hear from God Almighty. When you hear from God, you expect the words to be holy or something like that. But that was it. Those were the exact words He spoke to me, and there was no doubt in my mind that it was God. If the room had been filled with a hundred people, no one else would have heard it. He didn't speak in audible words to my head. He spoke directly to my spirit. It was so beautiful.

Well, needless to say, I was a bit excited. Actually, I went a bit bananas. Though it was close to 2:00 a.m., I had to share this experience with someone. Who better than my wife, Gail! So I ran to my bedroom and I proceeded to awaken my sweet, precious (and now pregnant) wife. I very gently placed my hand on her shoulder and said, "Honey, wake up."

A bit startled, and very sleepy, she opened her eyes and said, "What's wrong?"

"Honey, you're not gonna believe what just happened to me!" (Pause) "God just spoke to me! He spoke to me! To me! Gail, you're pregnant!"

I think I might have been a bit overanxious in telling her such startling news at that hour of the night. As I look back, I see that I probably could have chosen my words a little better. But how many men in the world ever have the opportunity to tell their wives the good news? Men are never the first to know. It's always the doctor, the mother, and then the father. I was in a very unique situation. As a matter of fact, the only other man I could find in this position dates all the way back to Abraham! Elizabeth and Mary both knew before their husbands!

After just being awakened from a deep sleep, all Gail could say was: "What?" So, I did what God did for me just minutes before. I repeated myself. "Gail, you're pregnant! God just told me that you're pregnant! We're gonna have a son!"

With a bit of indignation, Gail retorted, "Jeff, I'm not pregnant!"

"Yes you are! God just told me!"

She then said, "Jeff, I am not pregnant! Don't you think I would know if I was pregnant? I think you were probably dreaming."

Probably dreaming? I could not believe that she didn't believe me. "Gail, I wasn't dreaming. I was just on the floor in the living room and God spoke to me! He told me that you are pregnant!"

A little more disgusted with my persistence, she again said, "Jeff, I am definitely not pregnant! I know I'm not pregnant! I've been on the pill. I haven't missed my period, and I would know if I'm pregnant, and I'm definitely not!"

Seeing how upset she was becoming, I quickly said, "Okay, fine. Let's just go to sleep, and we can talk about it in the morning."

As I turned out the light, the last words she spoke to me that early April morning were, "There's nothing to talk about. I'm not pregnant!"

You must understand that we had already discussed that we wouldn't have any more children. We had Brent and Jeni. An older son, and a younger daughter. Perfect. A nice, wholesome All-American family. There's only one major detail that we forgot. God! Little did we know that He had other plans for our family. When the sun arose the next morning, I was up and at 'em, ready to begin the new day with my now pregnant wife. When she woke up, we began the day with the same conversation from several hours earlier. My wife thought I was losing my mind. As I look back on that wild and wonderful morning, I guess I can't really blame her. But you and I know better, don't we?

Being the man I was, I really didn't know what women had to go through to find out about this blessed event. If she wouldn't believe me, I knew she would believe her doctor. The trick was, how could I get her to go for a check-up to see if she was pregnant? When I arrived at my office, I shrewdly decided to take matters into my own hands. I picked up the phone and did the only thing I could think of. I called her doctor. The receptionist answered the phone with, "Dr. Miller's office, can I help you?"

"Yes," I said. "I would like to make an appointment."

The receptionist (probably thinking this was a practical joke) said, "Dr. Miller is a gynecologist, sir. Are you sure you have the right number?"

A little embarrassed, I said, "The appointment is not for me, it's for my wife."

We made the appointment for the following Friday. From that moment until the day of the appointment, I did not say one word about the situation.

The night before her appointment with Dr. Miller, Gail thought I was being so romantic. Actually I was just being sensitive to what I was about to put her through and covering all the bases. I made my sweet, darling, pregnant wife a nice bubble bath by candlelight. Poor Gail. She really did think I was being romantic, when in actuality I was being sneaky.

Fountain Hills is a beautiful community about twelve miles northeast of the Phoenix metropolitan area. Dr. Miller's office was about a fifteen mile drive. That Friday morning I said to Gail, "Come on, honey, let's go for a ride into town." I even suggested what she wear that day.

As we approached Dr. Miller's office, Gail looked at me with eyes ablaze and said, "Jeff, where are we going?"

"I made an appointment for you to see Dr. Miller. I figured since you didn't believe me, you would believe him when he tells you that you're pregnant."

She lost it as she said, "Jeff, you're out of your mind! I told you I'm not pregnant! This is ridiculous! You're crazy!"

There was the opening I was waiting for. "I'm crazy, huh? Okay, if I'm crazy, then you have to humor me. Well, then, humor me! Go into Dr. Miller's office and get checked. If Dr. Miller says you're not pregnant, then you can take me next door to the psychiatrist and have me checked out!"

I walked Gail into the office, which was wall-to-wall women. The only men in that office were Dr. Miller and me. I said, "Honey, while you're waiting here, I'm going to run to the office to pick up my paycheck." My office was just a few miles away, and I figured I could get back in plenty of time to be with Gail when she heard the good news from Dr. Miller. Little did I know that the other thing God spoke to me was about to come true.

When I arrived at my office to pick up my check, I was told that my boss wanted to see me. When I went into his office, he was pretty blunt as he said, "Jeff, I'm sorry I have to do this, but I'm going to have to let you go." As he said those words, my mind immediately went back to that morning several days before and the words I heard God speak: "You're going to lose your job in a week; your wife is pregnant; you're going to have a son."

"This is incredible!" I blurted out loud. "I can't believe this! You're firing me! I forgot. That's exactly what God told me was going to happen this week. This is incredible! I knew it! God really did speak to me! Gail really is pregnant!" By this time, the man who just fired me from a job I was miserable at was probably elated at knowing he just rid his company of a raving lunatic. At least by his standards. I could sense the angels having a blast at my jubilation. I could see them all sitting around getting a chuckle out of my exuberant reaction to just being fired and loving it, because I knew this man standing before me had no idea of the spiritual significance of what was taking place. I saw at that moment who was in control of my life. It wasn't man—it was God. Needless to say, I was excited. I still remember the bewildered look on his face as I thanked him for being obedient to what God had planned for me. He refused to accept the truth in what I tried to share with him about my relationship with the Lord. But nothing else mattered to me at that moment. I just wanted to get back to Gail so that we could rejoice together.

When I arrived at Dr. Miller's office, I was surprised to see Gail already finished and waiting outside for me. She was literally doing that old foot-tapping-with arms-folded routine. She had that "I'm-going-to-kill-you-for-putting-me-through-this" look in her eyes. What she did not have was that "Oh-gee-isn't-it-exciting-that-we're-going-to-have-another-child" look.

"Well, what happened? When are you due?" I asked expectantly, totally ignoring the look on her face.

"I'm not!" she responded rather coldly. "I told you, Jeff. I'm not pregnant. Now what was that about a psychiatrist?"

This is not possible, I thought to myself. I knew God had spoken to me. I had never heard His voice before, but I knew beyond a shadow of a doubt that I heard Him early that morning several days before. I couldn't believe she wasn't pregnant. "He made a mistake," I said.

"What? Are you kidding me? Dr. Miller did not make a mistake, Jeff. I'm just not pregnant. I told you, you were dreaming."

"I want to talk with him," I said. As I parked the car, I could see that Gail was furious. Her husband, the real estate salesman was about to go and tell her gynecologist that he made a mistake during his examination.

"You are not going to embarrass me, Jeff."

"Please, Gail. Please understand. I've got to be sure. I've got to know if I heard God speak to me the other night. Please. If Dr. Miller is certain, I promise you, I won't say another word about it. I just have to know." This precious, sensitive woman that God blessed me with could sense my desperation to know the truth. I had to confirm hearing God's voice. I already knew in my heart that I did.

Gail accompanied me back into the office. I walked over to the receptionist and said, "I'd like to speak with Dr. Miller." I guess it's not too often that a man asks to speak with the doctor, because she immediately escorted us to his office. We sat there for several minutes in total silence. When Dr. Miller finally came in, I did not mince any words. "Dr. Miller, is it possible that you made a mistake when you examined Gail? I mean, what if she conceived just a few days ago? Isn't it possible that it's too early for you to tell if she's pregnant with the test you do here?"

With a bewildered look on his face he said, "It's possible, Mr. Brodsky, but not very likely."

I then suggested a bit sheepishly, "Well, is there any other test that can be done to see if Gail has conceived?"

By this time, you could plainly see by the look on Gail's face that she was convinced I had completely lost control of my mind.

Dr. Miller said, "There is a test she could take, but you would have to go to the lab."

Without even so much as a glance over at Gail, I said, "Where exactly is the lab?" He informed me that the lab was down the hall and that the receptionist could call them and tell them we were coming over. I don't know if he was trying to get rid of me or if he was just intrigued by the story I had told him about how God told me Gail was pregnant.

Gail had now conceded to the fact that her husband was going all the way with this one. Walking down the corridor to the lab, I said to Gail, "I give you my solemn word, honey. This is it. If they say no, I'll admit I was wrong. I promise." Gail did not even acknowledge my speaking to her. It was as if she was in a trance.

After the tests at the lab were over, we drove home in silence. All we could hear was the praise tape playing in the car. I still hadn't told her about losing my job. I was afraid she would do something drastic. After all, I was the only one who was totally elated about all that was happening.

About three hours later our telephone rang. It was the lab with the results of the test. When they told me that Gail was about two weeks pregnant, all I could do was weep. I handed her the phone so she could hear the news for herself. She was completely overwhelmed. Totally speechless. Motionless. She was also very humble. She came directly over to where I was sitting and weeping. As she apologized, she embraced me and together we sat and wept. The tears were joyful. We both knew at that moment that our God had spoken to me.

Several weeks passed, and then a thought occurred to me. Why? Why did God tell me Gail was pregnant? There had to be a reason. Obviously, we would have found out sooner or later. Why did God tell me the way He did? The answer came to me after our first bill arrived from Dr. Miller. While Gail was in the doctor's office I was still employed. As a result, the entire medical bill for the birth of our son

Lance was taken care of by the insurance I had with the company that fired me. If we had waited even one more hour for Gail's appointment with Dr. Miller on that wild and wonderful day, none of the medical bills would have been covered by the type of insurance we had.

I was fortunate enough to be in the delivery room at that special moment when Lance was coming into the world. I told Dr. Miller that it was definitely a boy. When he asked, "What if it's a girl?" I reminded him of that day in his office almost nine months ago and of how I knew. If it was going to be a girl, then God changed His mind. If He did, He would have told me first, as He knew that I had told so many friends of that night when He first spoke to me.

From the moment God spoke to me in the wee hours of that early April morning, I knew Lance was going to be a special child. It would take fourteen years and Lance's insight to teach me something that would astound me. I was speaking to Lance's youth group one Sunday morning in December of 1992. Lance had just turned fourteen. Just as I was about to share my prepared message, God told me to share the story of how Lance was born. My first thought was, "No way!" I had never shared the story with the youth before. Besides, it would really embarrass Lance. Yet I couldn't dismiss the inner knowing that God was very definitely telling me to share the story; so I did.

As I told the story, I was amazed at the expressions on the faces of these young people. After all, I was telling this wild story about one of their own. This miracle child was in the room with us, and as I spoke, the young people continually glanced over at Lance with looks of amazement and wonder in their eyes. The looks on their faces were priceless. Their response was wonderful.

When I finished speaking, Lance and I walked to the car together. Our conversation was mind-boggling. "I hope I didn't embarrass you, son."

"No way, Dad," he said. "I like it when you tell that story. It makes me feel special. We're in good company, you know. Did you know that God only told four people about a child being born before it happened? The first one was Abraham, when He told him about Isaac. Abraham and Isaac were the first two people who were told by God about the coming Messiah. The next one was Elizabeth. She was giving birth to the one (John, The Baptist) who would tell the people that Jesus was coming. Then God spoke to Mary and Joseph and told them about Jesus. The next one God spoke to is you. Maybe I'm the one God wants to tell people about The Second Coming of Jesus."

I'll never forget what I felt inside when he said those words to me. Do I believe that Lance is "**the**" messenger for Jesus' Second Coming? No. But I do believe he is "**a**" messenger, along with the thousands of teens I see on fire all around the world today. There's a spiritual revival like never before, and it's happening in the lives of our youth.

On the drive home, all I could think about was the miracle of God speaking to me fourteen years earlier to tell me that Lance was to be born. I also remembered the first night he was in our home. After everyone else was asleep, I took Lance from his crib and walked out into the cool December night. As I held Lance in my hands, I looked up toward the innumerable stars that shone brightly overhead. I lifted this tiny, precious gift God had entrusted into my care toward the heavens and committed myself to raise him to love the One who had given him life.

Before you were born I sanctified you;
and I ordained you a prophet to the nations."
Jeremiah 1:5

CHAPTER THREE

THE CREATOR OF ALL CHILDREN

As a result of the circumstances surrounding the birth of Lance, I learned some meaningful truths about creation. After his birth, I did an intensive study on creation. The following passages of Scripture became alive to me as I saw the truth in what God was saying.

Job 31:15
Did not **He who made me in the womb** make them? Did not the same One fashion us in the womb?

Psalm 127:3
Behold, children are a heritage from the LORD, **the fruit of the womb** is a reward.

Psalm 139:13
For You formed my inward parts; You covered me **in my mother's womb.**

Isaiah 44:2
Thus says the LORD **who made you and formed you from the womb,** who will help you: 'Fear not, O Jacob My servant; and you, Jeshurun, whom I have chosen.'

Isaiah 44:24
Thus says the LORD, your Redeemer, and **He who formed you from the womb:** "I am the LORD, who makes all things, Who stretches out the heavens all alone, Who spreads abroad the earth by Myself."

Isaiah 49:5

And now the LORD says, **Who formed Me from the womb** to be His Servant...

Jeremiah 1:5

Before I formed you in the womb I knew you; before you were born I sanctified you; I ordained you a prophet to the nations.

Is it a coincidence that He chose to state to us so many times that He is the Creator? I think not. It seems to me that He truly wanted us to remember this awesome truth about Him. I'm so grateful that He gave us those constant reminders throughout the Scriptures. From them I gained a new awareness as to Who the Creator actually is. I've come to thoroughly understand that God is **The** Creator. We are His creation. Did you get that? HIS creation! We are the tools He chose to use to create His design for humankind.

Have you ever noticed that a tool alone can do nothing without the hands of its creator? Each artist uses their tools to meticulously form, polish, shape, and refine what they are creating — until it's perfect in their eyes. The potter uses her hands along with mud, clay, and other tools of her trade to shape the pottery that will become her finished work of art. The sculptor chisels, carves, hews, and shapes his chosen material to create the sculpture already within him. The artist's tools consist of a palette of colors in one hand, a brush in the other. He'll mix the colors of paint that will be used to create life on canvas. The musician's tool will be the instrument of choice to create a myriad of music. Likewise, God uses man and woman as His tools to create His children. Just as each individual artist's work of art is different, so is each one of God's creations.

Colossians 1:16

For by Him all things were created that are in heaven and that are on earth, visible and invisible, whether thrones or dominions or principalities or powers. All things were created through Him and for Him.

The fact that God is the Creator of all things is undeniable if you believe the Bible to be the infallible Word of God. This being true, why can't we learn to accept and love one another unconditionally? Why, as His creation, is it so difficult to see each man, woman, and child as His? I stand amazed at how ignorant we are to the truth of who and what we are as God's creation.

When we behold the magnitude and magnificence of the creation of a human being, and come to a sincere understanding of the privilege we have of being used by our Creator as His tool to bring the miracle of life He's blessed us with into the world, then we can begin to grasp the enormous responsibility He's given us in training that child to become all that He has created our son or daughter to be—as a future man or woman of God. We can also then look at any of His creation with eyes of love and a heart of acceptance, regardless of their race, nationality, color, or religious preference.

1 John 4:10-11

In this is love, not that we loved God, but that He loved us and sent His Son to be the propitiation for our sins. Beloved, if God so loved us, we also ought to love one another.

With His love, we can accept anyone, whether it is a newborn babe or a ninety-year-old. As we grasp the truth of God being the Creator of all of us, we will then see each person on this earth as His, with the potential of serving and loving Him. Hopefully, we can then grasp what it means to love one another—unconditionally. Not loving "if"—but "because." All throughout our lives we're taught through the actions and words of others that love is conditional. We hear it from parents, siblings, friends, teachers, classmates, and co-workers. I'll love you if you're pretty, if you're handsome, if you get good grades, if you make the football team, if you become a cheerleader, if you give yourself to me physically, if you dress a certain way, if you succeed financially, if you climb the corporate ladder, if you let me have my own way—the list goes on and on. I'm so blessed to know that God is not like that. He doesn't love us "if"—He simply loves us "because."

We need to see each other through the eyes of love that He has for each of His creation. When we do, then we'll be able to love each other unconditionally. He loves us because we're His creation. We need to have that same kind of love for the creation He's blessed us with.

For some reason, God chose Gail and me to raise our children. His creations. He entrusted them into our care. I'm sure He knew what He was doing when He made the choice. The same applies to you. Of all the parents God could have chosen to be the ones to raise your child, you're the one He gave the responsibility and privilege to. I do not believe you would have been given that opportunity, responsibility, and privilege if God didn't think you could do it.

I also believe that He has equipped you with all the necessary tools to accomplish the job. What you do with those tools, though, is entirely up to you. God obviously saw something in you that showed Him you are capable of completing the task set before you. Now it is your decision as to how much effort you are willing to put into that task.

The only difference between the mediocre and the master is that one decided to put more effort into his or her training and understanding of how to use the talents, tools, and gifts that he or she's been given. I've seen people with the same skills, yet one goes much further with their gifts and talents than the other. You see it in every area of life. The athlete who enjoys the game to a certain level, but is not willing to put in the extra effort it takes to become a champion. The gold medal goes to another who did. The musician who's satisfied with what he knows, instead of what he could be. The artist who can paint a moderate painting, while a masterpiece lies dormant within. The composer who's satisfied with swaying his arms to the music, instead of creating the symphony that swirls deep within his soul.

I love to fish. Other than sharing my faith or being with my family, fishing is what I truly love to do—summer, winter (yes, Colorado winter), spring, or fall. Whether I'm on a calm, pristine lake, walking along a clear, tree-lined river or stream, or on a fishing boat out in the vastness of the ocean, I love all kinds of fishing. I especially love ice-fishing. I sincerely enjoy sitting on a bucket in the middle of winter in sub-zero weather with my two to four pound test ice fishing line over a seven-inch hole just waiting for one of those beautiful crappie or perch to take a bite out of my tiny tear-drop, maggot-tipped lure. I remember the first time I went. It was at Cherry Creek Reservoir in Colorado. There was an oldtimer named Don who sat a few feet from me. Every time he dropped his line, he hooked a crappie. Ten times in a row!

I could not understand when I went fishing why there would always be those few fishermen like Don who would catch their limit almost every time. I saw so many other so-called fishermen go home empty-handed (like me). A few would go home with one or two, but there were always those few who would leave with a stringer full of fish. We were all fishing the same waters. We all had basically the same gear. Why did some leave with so much more? Why do twenty percent of the fishermen catch eighty percent of the fish? I wanted to know—so I asked. I didn't ask the ones who went home empty-handed. I already knew how to do that. I asked those who always had a good catch. I asked people like Don. Within three minutes of asking Don his secret for catching fish through the ice, I had my first one hooked! The fish was hooked, and so was I! I then began to study fishing techniques from the masters. I watched fishing programs, began putting together a fishing library of books and videos, and slowly but surely I became one of those few who I used to watch with envy. I am now one of those who can go home with my stringer full, catching my limit almost every time. I basically used the same tools as before (with a few new additions), but now I was using them the way they were created to be used.

The same goes for you as a parent. God did not give any greater skills, knowledge, or understanding as to how to raise a child to only a select few. He gave you the same inherent, natural instincts of parenting that He gave to everyone else. You have the same parenting tools available to you as any parent that ever lived.

He gave you the same heart of love and desire to train your child properly as He did for every parent. But due to circumstances in your life that molded and shaped you into the person you are today, you have a different personal outlook and understanding as to the proper way to parent your child. So do I. The difference with me was that I was never satisfied with what I had. I wanted to know more about what I could do to help my children become all God created them to be. With all my heart, I wish I knew twenty years ago what I know today.

My children are all grown. But the hunger within me to learn parenting skills has never died. My children will always be my children. As a result of what I've learned, I can continue to help them learn as they become parents to my future grandchildren. One of the greatest desires of my heart is that you will benefit from the years of research and study I've put into this area. I know that the principles learned from this book will not only help you to be a better prepared and more informed parent, but it will also benefit your children as well. You do not have to wait until your children are grown to understand how to raise them properly. God has given you tools to use today to help you train your children the way they are to go.

As I thought about what Lance said to me in that synagogue about wanting "to be a man," I was overcome with these questions:

- What was I doing to train my son for his passage into adulthood?
- How was I helping him to become the man of God that He created him to be?
- Why did I put away the traditions of my heritage?
- What actually were my responsibilities as a Christian father?
- Why is there no "rite of passage" in Christianity?

It was this last question that gnawed deep within me.

PART TWO

The Journey
Into Adulthood

CHAPTER FOUR

"OH THE TIMES,
THEY 'DEFINITELY' ARE A CHANGIN'"

Where or when in our children's lives are they taught to deal with the pressures they experience each day? What they usually hear from adults is, "It's no different today than when I was a kid. We had the same pressures as you kids today." That thinking is wrong, wrong, wrong! The pressures that our young people are under today are greater than in any other time in modern history.

"Youth are so different now than they were in the past." Have you ever heard that? Or said it? Read the words of this philosopher:

"There is little doubt that the present generation of young men and women in College is in serious moral difficulty. Compared with generations preceding, they have shunned discipline and a willingness to excel in their studies. Many give little or no thought to the serious issues of life. Common decency and modesty in manners and dress apparently are things of the past. The fact that evil is called good while good is called evil seems to be of small concern to them. Student groups indulge in wild orgies of self-gratification while coeds dress and walk in a manner deliberately intended to arouse sexual desire. Both young men and women in their actions and conversations make sexual overtures in the most shameless fashion..."

Does this sound like a fair description of our youth today? That was written by the Greek philosopher Aristophanes—some 500 years before the birth of Christ.

Another philosopher comments:

"Our youth today love luxury. They have bad manners, contempt for authority, and disrespect for older people. Children today are tyrants! They no longer rise when their elders enter the room. They contradict their parents, chatter before visitors, gobble their food and tyrannize their teachers."

Another accurate description of today's teenager. This quote was written by Socrates in 5 B.C.

History shows us that today's generation is no more righteous or rotten than any other young people before—the same problems reoccur in each era. Young people are no worse than before, or better, but unfortunately just as bad.[1] Yet, there are some things that are uniquely different about this generation of young people that have NEVER been true about youth at any time in history. They face pressures and problems that no other generation has ever had to face. And they face them at a time unlike any other generation.

Parents, teachers, and youth workers need to open their eyes and wake up to the times we're living in. Bob Dylan's song was both poetic and prophetic when he penned the words of his song *The Times, They are a Changin'*. He challenged parents to avoid criticizing the elements of a society they cannot understand. But instead he urged them to come alongside their children and lend their wisdom and experience.

Without a doubt there were teenage gangs around during the '50s and '60s, but not with the attitude and demeanor of today's gangs. The gangs in my day were not the threat they are now. There's a much greater degree of violence today, and young people are made to feel more threatened for not joining a gang. Violence permeates every aspect of a young person's life. It's on our televisions, in hundreds of video games, in the movies, in schools, and especially in music. They even have their own style of music in the form of what's appropriately called "Gangsta Rap." In many of the songs the messages of violence are clear. I was originally planning to quote some of the words to songs recorded by people such as Dr. Dre, Domino, Ice T, Out Cold Cops and the like, but the lyrics were so rough and laced with profanity, degradation, racial epithets, and violent threats I decided not to.

This genre of violent entertainment is illustrated by rap music star Tupac Shakur, whose lyrics about crime and violence in the black ghetto often mirrored his own troubled life. He died on September 13, 1996, as he and a record company executive were shot in a "gangland" style murder while driving in Las Vegas, Nevada.

I have been absolutely astonished at some of the music that Christian youth listen to today. Many of today's parents have taken a less active role in the choices they allow their children to make—with devastating consequences.

It is astounding what is available for the enemy to use as a tool to destroy the lives of thousands of kids. With the push of a button at a home computer, pornography is more easily available than at any time in history. It's simple for a child to escape into the World Wide Web, since most parents have chosen to be ignorant to this new method of destruction. Now, don't get me wrong moms and dads—I use this same weapon (the computer) that I'm talking about. But with any weapon today, it can be constructive or destructive. It all depends on who taught the user of the weapon how to use it. In many homes today it's the children teaching the adults how to use computer technology. If you're going to have a computer in your home, then have a basic understanding of how to use it yourself. This is crucial when it comes to entering into the world of what's known as the "information superhighway," the Internet, or the World Wide Web.

The age of the "information superhighway" has made our young people more intelligent in so many areas, but they still lack a great deal of understanding on how to cope with the problems and pressures of those who have come to be known as Generation X. Isn't it interesting that "X" is known in the Greek as a symbol for Christ? It comes from the Greek spelling of Christ or *Xristos*.

Things have changed drastically in the past one hundred years. Consider the enormous changes in two areas: communications and media. I recently learned while visiting with a friend who is an employee of TCI (Tele-Communications Inc.), one of the world's largest cable companies, that the city of Aurora, Colorado, will be a test site for a cable network with 500 channels! As of the publishing of this book, such a system is already in place in several cities across America and via satellite systems available around the world.

The Internet and World Wide Web now give us instant access to the entire world. You can book air travel, hotels, car-rentals, send flowers, purchase stocks, as well as buy groceries, pay your bills, and literally purchase anything you can think of from your home computer! Computers have literally changed the way we do banking as well as conduct business. Everything in our society has become instant. Mail as we know it is slowly changing to e-mail, where you can send a letter (or manuscript) instantly to whoever has a computer. If you do not have a computer, just go to the grocery store and you can fax your document instantly. Overnight Express mail is still an option too. How about drive-thru banking, drive-thru meals, or if you are feeling a bit tired and hungry you can have piping hot pizza delivered to your door in about a half hour.

Today's generation has no need to ever leave the house. They can be entertained by watching a myriad of television programs twenty-four hours a day, rent a movie (even have it delivered), play video games for hours on end, or "chat" with someone they've never met from Hong Kong via one of the many "on-line" services available today. Instant gratification.

Parents today say: "If my child needs something, I'll just get it for him. If I can't afford it—no problem (or no worries in Australia), I can get "instant credit.""

Parents, now hear this:

Children Need Your Presence Not Your Presents!

When Diane came to my office with her then fourteen-year-old daughter Jamie, she was frazzled. Jamie had just been expelled from the eighth grade. As was my practice, I had Diane come into my office first. She was beside herself.

"Pastor Jeff, I can't believe what's happened. Jamie was expelled from school today!"

"Why?" I asked.

"The principal called me in and told me that Jamie was using vulgar language in the school to other students as well as other teachers. I was also told that the principal was informed that Jamie was seen smoking in the schoolyard, and acting promiscuously around the boys. Pastor Jeff, I cannot believe that about Jamie. She's only fourteen!"

Jamie was not a part of my regular youth group, so I didn't know much about her. Diane had attended our church a few times, so she had no one to turn to but me. I asked her a series of questions that even surprised me as they came out of my mouth. "Diane, let me ask you something. Can you tell me the names of your daughter's five closest friends?"

"I don't know all her friends' names. She has a lot of friends."

"Can you tell me the names of her four favorite television programs?"

"She watches a lot of TV. I don't know what she watches. She's usually up in her room."

"How about her three favorite musical groups or favorite radio stations?"

"She listens to music all the time. She has a huge collection of tapes. I don't know the names of them! What does this have to do with anything?"

I now knew Jamie's problem. After having Jamie come in, I asked her the same questions I had asked her mom. She answered them without hesitation. She was listening to music that was straight from the pit. She was watching television programs that did nothing but feed her wrong information about relationships. Her friends did not attend church. Jamie had no positive influence in her life in any area. I asked Jamie to send her mom in again.

When Diane came back in and sat down, I said, "Tell me something Diane. If Jamie was a drug addict, would you be her pusher?"

"What! What are you talking about? Jamie's not on drugs, is she?"

"No, I didn't say that. I just want to know, if she was, would you be her pusher?"

"Of course not!" she said.

"Why not?" I asked.

"Well, because it would hurt her."

"How would it hurt her?" I asked.

"It would hurt her physically, and it could damage her mind too."

"That's right, Diane. I believe that's what's happening to Jamie. Her mind is being destroyed by the programs she's watching on television, as well as the music she's listening to, and the friends she has are hurting her as well. Diane, who bought the TV that Jamie watches?"

"I did," came the response.

"What about the stereo in her room? The tapes she listens to? The electricity for all of it? The money to go out with her friends to see movies? Who pays for all of it?"

"Well, I do..." she said hesitantly.

"Diane, these things are all things that hurt Jamie and are being used to destroy her mind. They're just like a drug, and you're the one paying for all of it. That's what I mean about being her pusher."

As the difficult lesson of what I was trying to get across set in, Diane sat in the chair and wept. After we prayed together, I had Jamie come back in and talked with both of them about right decisions and choices that needed to be made immediately.

It is absolutely mind-boggling and frightening when you look at our past one hundred years in just ten-year intervals. The beginning of the century gave us the Industrial Revolution, and with that World War I. The 1920s offered us the beginning of radio, the invention of the TV, the Roaring '20s, and the stock market crash and gangsters. The '30s had the world in a deep depression along with the emergence of Nazism. The '40s are known as The War Years. The '50s are best remembered as the introduction to rock & roll. The '60s brought us the Vietnam War, peace movement and hippie generation. The '70s gave us disco, satellite TV and the invention of the micro-processor computer on a chip. On to the '80s and the introduction of cable TV, the IBM PC, cell phones, and Valley Girl mentality. Now we're in the final stages of the '90s, which have given us so far Gangsta Rap, a computer in every home and Generation X-ers.

Each previous generation was so very different than the preceding one. And as we "progressed," it seems that the attitudes and lifestyles of our youth have digressed. As you look back over the last one hundred years, I'm sure you'll agree that things have gotten progressively worse. Take for example the area of education. In many public schools today, armed guards or police roam the hallways. Many schools now have metal detectors that students have to pass through prior to entering the building. Hello! Is anybody out there? Is anybody taking notice that we have a generation of incredibly violent teenagers?

If you read the papers or watch the news, I'm sure you've noticed the number of drive-by shootings. Teenagers are being hauled off to prison in record numbers. They attack both other students as well as teachers in the classroom. As early as one previous generation (a generation being recognized as forty years), in 1956, one of the greatest problems in the classroom was gum-chewing! Look what's happened in just one generation!

We've heard it stated for years that we're living in the last days. Are we? You won't hear a definitive, absolute answer from me. What I do know is what I see as a sign of the times according to what I read in the Scriptures. Are we raising the generation that will usher in the Second Coming of Jesus? Maybe. Perhaps we're raising the generation that will raise the generation who will usher in the coming of Christ. I don't know. This present generation is vastly different from any other generation in history, and the enemy seems to be doing everything possible to destroy today's (and as a result, tomorrow's) youth. He has waged the greatest all-out attack since the Exodus. Why now? Consider this.

I believe we are in what people are calling the computer age. Just several years ago we were in the industrial age and about one hundred years ago, we were in the agricultural age. From the agricultural age and prior, fathers were at home with their families all day. The only time he left the home was usually to go hunting. When he did that, his son(s) would go with him. Children had both parents available for their upbringing, teaching, discipling, discipline, counsel, guidance, and direction for their lives. Then along comes the industrial age in the early 1900s. Almost overnight, fathers were taken out of the home in droves all over the world, especially in primary (like the United States) and other developing nations. Home life as it had been known for thousands of years prior to the industrial age had now dramatically changed. Mothers were placed in a position they were not created for. All of a sudden they had to be both mother and father to their children in the absence of the father. The mentoring that took place on a daily basis had become a once or twice a week task when Dad was available on weekends.

As a result of fathers being absent from the home, mothers also had to be the disciplinarian in the family. A mother's arms were made to caress and nurture a child after the discipline by Dad. Now they had become the arms that meted out the discipline. While a father was home prior to the industrial age, there were few discipline problems because the child knew that Dad's discipline was swift and fair. A new set of rules would be thought up by the industrial age teen as he saw that he could get away with much more with Dad gone. He could easily get past his mother's softness. She was much more forgiving than Dad. She was created with that tenderness and gentleness. So after an infraction, the scenario in many homes probably went like this:

Mom: "Son, you know that you weren't supposed to do that. I'm going to have to tell Dad when he gets home."

Son: "I'm sorry, Mom. Please don't tell Dad. I promise I'll never do it again. If you tell Dad, he's going to punish me. Please don't tell."

Sound familiar? It still goes on today. It all began not more than a hundred years ago at the advent of the industrial age. Prior to this time, Dad was already home, and the infraction would have been dealt with swiftly and firmly.

Another change happened in the structure of the family. After a hard day at work, a father would come home ready to greet his children. But when he would call for them, they wouldn't come out because they were hiding. Mom would greet Dad by saying, "Honey, the children did this today and they did that. Take care of them." All of a sudden, Dad wasn't so "dear" anymore.

What I'm seeing today, though, is a turnaround within the home life. With the emergence of the Men's Movement across the land, attitudes and adjustments are being made in thousands of families. It's taken a while (really, only about one hundred years), but fathers are seeing the importance of their roles and are taking seriously the responsibility for their actions as the head of the household.

As we find ourselves in the nucleus of the computer age, I believe we are seeing the fulfillment of the prophecy found in Malachi 4:5-6:

"Behold, I will send you Elijah the prophet before the coming of the great and dreadful day of the LORD. And he will turn the hearts of the fathers to the children, and the hearts of the children to their fathers, lest I come and strike the earth with a curse."

These are the final words written in the Old Testament. Since the early 1900s, we have seen the fulfillment of these prophetic words within the church across our land. In each twenty-year period the church has seen the rise of revivalists, healers, teachers, pastors, and apostles. In this decade it seems we have seen a strong influx of prophets. Is this mere coincidence? Or are we really seeing a fulfillment of Malachi's prophecy?

In the midst of today's computer age is another fulfillment of this Scripture. The hearts of the fathers are being
turned to the children. Consider this fact. About ten years
ago (based on a study from *Home Office Computing* magazine and IDC/Link, a New York based research firm), there
were approximately 300,000 parents who worked from home
in America. Just ten years later that number has jumped
more than 100 times to 42,000,000! That number is rapidly
growing on a daily basis, as even large companies are seeing
the benefits of allowing their employees to work from home
because of the enhancements and advances in the computer as a communications tool.

Many of today's violent teens were yesterday's "latch-
key kids." These were the children who grew up by the mil-
lions with no parents to care for them after school. As a
result of parents working from home, and the increase in
home-schooling, we're seeing a new generation of children
with stronger values and better self-images.

It is our responsibility as their parents to do everything
we can with the tools God has given us to help these children become all that God has created them to be as they
grow and mature into young men and women.

I believe with all my heart that one of the greatest missing elements in raising children in Christianity today is the
lack of the "rite of passage," where we recognize in a ceremony, then celebrate together as our child steps into adulthood.

 CHAPTER FIVE

The Cry for Help: A War Called Suicide

While ministering to adult singles at a church in Phoenix, I remember a call coming in the middle of the night. Awakened out of a deep sleep I answered the phone. The voice on the other end said, "Jeff, this is (name withheld). I can't take it anymore. I'm ending it tonight."

I responded in a bit of an unorthodox way. "What are you calling me for? Do you want me to do your funeral?" There was a lengthy silence between us.

Finally, the caller said, "Well... no."

"Then why'd you call me?" I asked. "Do you want me to stop you from killing yourself? Do you want me to talk you out of doing it? Okay. Don't do it! Obviously, you really don't want to take your life or you wouldn't be calling me, unless you're calling to say good-bye. You and I both know that's not the case. So get some sleep, and call me tomorrow morning."

The way I figured it, the caller really didn't want to take her life. If she did, I wouldn't have received that call. I would have gotten a call from someone else, telling me that the deed was done. I'm not a psychiatrist, nor am I a psychologist or psycho-analyst (and I don't pretend to or want to be). At the time I was just a pastor who cared about people (especially those who were a part of my flock). I've been taught to share the truth in love. That's exactly what I did. I met with the caller the next morning, and after talking for a couple of hours and some prayer, everything was fine. She came to see that she had quite a bit to live for. All she needed was a listening ear and a caring heart. That was nearly fifteen years ago and I'm happy to say that she is still alive and doing well.

Much of the distress of today's young people results in a cry for help. They are bombarded by a society that says they are ugly, inadequate, and unloveable. Unfortunately, many conclude that suicide is the solution. In fact, there is a spiritual war going on for their lives. We must be prepared to do battle against the one who seeks to destroy the life of the children that God has entrusted to us. "Be sober, be vigilant; because your adversary the devil walks about like a roaring lion, seeking whom he may devour." (1 Peter 5:8)

When a sixteen-year-old Christian youth in our church committed suicide several years ago, it devastated me. I've been through so much anguish in my own life, but no matter how hopeless the situation may have appeared at the time—suicide was never an option, never even a thought. I've had my share (like so many others) of mental anguish, despair, depression, and pain; but the thought of taking my own life has never (and I mean never) been an option. At the time I could not understand how a young person could come to such a state of mind where they would even consider suicide—let alone actually follow through with it. To take one's own life was something that was (and still is) beyond my comprehension. It disturbed me when someone so young took his or her life. I had to know more about the subject. Was suicide among teenagers in America really at epidemic proportions? I began researching teen suicide in America. The statistics were unbelievable and shocking! Much of the following results were taken from an extensive study by The George H. Gallup International Institute as well as additional research I did from various resources.

SOME DISTURBING FACTS ABOUT TEENS IN TODAY'S WORLD

• Suicide is considered to be the #1 killer among teens in America today. It was originally thought that accidents were the #1 cause, until further study revealed that many of the "accidents" were attempted suicides.

• Suicide is the leading cause of death for 13-19 year-olds.

• Suicide attempts among youth has risen **more than 300** percent since the 1950s.

• Over **250,000** teenagers will attempt suicide **this year.**

• One fifth of teenagers in America today have come close to committing suicide or have actually attempted to.

• For every teen who commits suicide, at least 100 others attempt it.

• 90 percent of teen suicides occur at home between 3:00 p.m. and midnight.

• 93 percent of suicidal teens reported a lack of communication between them and their parents.

• The statistics are even worse per capita in Australia.

WHY SUICIDE?

People don't just wake up one day and say, "What a horrible day, I think I'll kill myself." From what I've found in my research, most people who commit suicide have thought about it for quite some time. Their response to circumstances and situations in their life brings them to a point of desperation, where they sincerely believe there is no escape from their situation—except to end their life. Listed here are some of the main reasons given for suicide attempts. These are based on notes left by the victims, as well as from interviews with many who had attempted, but succeeded—by failing:

THE TOP SIXTEEN REASONS FOR THOUGHTS OF SUICIDE

The main reasons given by teens:

Family Problems	Depression
Low Self Esteem	Problems With Friends
Life in General	School Problems
Boy/Girl Relations	Felt No One Cared
Drugs and Alcohol	Lack of Purpose

Pressure to Succeed   Stress
Confusion   Self-Doubt

The statistics on teenage pregnancy, illiteracy, drug and alcohol use, violence, crime, rape, sexually transmitted diseases (STDs) and gangs are just as staggering.

I consider all of the above to be "diseases" among our society that all have a common connection. If you'll notice, each one of these diseases (with the exception of AIDS and herpes as an STD) is totally curable! All it takes to cure any one of these diseases is education, motivation, and inspiration.

TWO QUESTIONS THAT MUST BE ANSWERED

I believe that each one of these dilemmas is directly related to the "Rite of Passage" or "Stepping Into Adulthood." How can a young person deal with some of the above issues if they're continually told they're still a child.

People, especially youth, need to have the answers to the following two questions: "Who am I?" and "Where am I going?" Notice that each of the reasons for suicide I've shown above can be directly related to either one's destiny or identity. This is no coincidence. It's an area that every child (as well as every adult) needs to be aware of.

In his book *The Ancient Paths*, Craig Hill talks about God's message throughout the Scriptures of identity and destiny.

IDENTITY: "To Me you are very valuable and are worth the life of Jesus Christ. You are a 'somebody.' You do belong here. Before the foundation of the earth, I planned for you. You were no mistake."

DESTINY: "You are destined to a great purpose on this earth. I placed you here for a purpose. You are a success as a person and are completely adequate and suited to carry out My purpose. Set your vision high, and allow Me to complete great accomplishments in your life."[1]

I believe that it is the responsibility of the parent (that's right, you!) to help guide their children in gaining an understanding of these two vital areas. They have a need to know their:

IDENTITY:
• As a member of God's family.

What is their role in the church? Do our children have to wait to become an adult member of the church before they have an opportunity to be recognized as a functioning, vital member of the church community?

• As a member of their earthly family.

What position have they been given within the family? What age must they become before they have the respect of their parents as a decision-maker in the family, where their opinion counts for something? Does it happen after they leave the home and become married adults? Or will they always be looked at as a child?

• As a member of society.

Society says we can be looked upon as an "adult" member of society when we become at least eighteen years old. We can then vote. In some states you can buy alcohol and cigarettes. During a time of war, you can also be drafted into the military.

I find it strange what society in general considers to be an adult, when compared to how God created us. I can't understand that God would create us to have all the necessary "tools" for adulthood, yet the society in which we live says we have to wait until a certain date to be recognized as an adult member of that society.

Our young people have the desire, as well as the fire that burns within, and no place to let it glow. When a fire gets out of control it can be very destructive. Just look at the fire that rages within the hearts of teens who join gangs. The "gang" has taken the place of the family, where the teen is recognized by a group of their peers as the "adult" he or she longs to be.

Helping your child understand their identity as a vital, significant member of society will give them the confidence needed to take their first steps into adulthood. The same thing happened when you taught your child to take his or her first steps. A "passage" took place when she walked toward you for the first time as your baby became a toddler. The process of learning to take those first steps was slow. The same should apply in walking your child from adolescence to adulthood. Slowly, they will begin to assimilate their role in that society as you help to guide them into understanding their identity as the man or woman of God He longs for them to be.

DESTINY:
- Why am I here?

Why did God see the need to create me? Haven't you ever wondered the same thing? What a great discussion to have with your child. Help them to see that God has a marvelous destiny for their life.
- Where am I going?

What lies ahead in my future? Teens today have a myriad of things that they think about relating to their future. They live in a world of uncertainty, where anything can happen at any given moment. Help bring stability into their lives by showing them that God has a definite path for their life that leads to an attainable goal in His plan for them.
- What is my purpose?

Hosea 4:6 says: "For lack of knowledge my people perish." There is a strong need to know one's purpose and direction in life, especially in the case of youth. Each one of us has that need to know why we were given life on this earth. Spend time praying with and for your child so that they clearly understand that God has a special purpose for them.

CHRISTIANITY IS MISSING OUT

I began to research the "rite of passage" in various cultures, societies, religions, and people groups throughout the world. Almost every one that I studied had some form of passage for their boys to become men and for their girls to become women. A *"rite"* or *"celebration"* takes place to commemorate this wonderful time in a child's life. In many societies there was a continual training and preparation for the *"passing on"* from childhood to adolescence to adulthood. During my research I was shocked that the only people not doing anything in this area was modern Christianity! We do nothing to help our boys understand the responsibilities and joys of passing on to manhood. And we fail to celebrate the passing on to womanhood for our girls. There's no rite, no celebration, no ceremony—**Nothing!**

I believe this lack has a direct correlation to the dilemma of teenage suicides in our country and the falling away of so many young men and women from the church to the world. Christianity has the highest "mortality rate" among its teens in relation to the faith of their upbringing! By Christianity here, I'm talking about all areas of Christianity: Catholics, Protestants, Evangelicals, Charismatics. The faith of many teens brought up in Christianity "dies" as they get older. More teens brought up in Christianity fall away from the faith of their parents than any other religious group in the world today. This is based on the five major religions in the world today—Christianity, Muslim, Hindu, Judaism and Buddhist.[2] Each one of these major religions has a deep history rooted in traditions. Many of those traditions involve the training of their children with a celebration and recognition at some point in their teen years when they are looked at as adult members in their cultures and societies. All of them except Christianity do something to celebrate this wonderful time in the young person's life. Why don't we? I believe it has become obvious, based on what I see in the lives of our youth today—the deep longing they have for that recognition.

Today's youth are crying out in desperation to a world that doesn't hear their screams. "Who am I?" "What am I?" "When will they treat me like a man (or woman)?" "When can I make decisions on my own?"

The one decision a young person makes that no one can stop is the decision to take his or her own life.

I believe a simple ceremony of recognition, along with training and discipleship in the area of teaching our young people the responsibilities of Christian adulthood, will help a great deal to alleviate what has become an epidemic in our society—taking the "easy" way out of a life of turmoil by suicide.

Suicide has become a "glorious" way to go among young people today. Many see these dead teens as heroes. Many who have committed suicide do so because of role models such as the late Kurt Cobain. While researching the topic of suicide on the Internet, I found almost 12,000 references to Kurt Cobain alone. Many of the references to him were in tribute to one who is looked upon as a "hero" to many of today's teens. This twenty-seven-year-old rock star took his life in April 1994 by sticking a loaded 20-gauge shotgun in his mouth and pulling the trigger. He did this after leaving a suicide note sharing his frustrations about his life and ending the note by telling his wife, Courtney Love, how much he loved her and his children. He became a martyr to many Generation X'rs, leading the way to a rash of "copycats." These imitators performed their final act by following the lead of a mentally disturbed, drug-crazed young man who had never been taught the responsibilities that come with "perceived" success.

If our youth are not taught properly, many of them will deal with their situation in the same inappropriate ways. Drug and alcohol abuse among children are at an alarming rate throughout the world. So is suicide. Why shouldn't they take the "easy" way out, when they have no idea as to the joys of overcoming their fears and frustrations?

How many parents "drown" their sorrows in a bottle? Then when they are inebriated they take it out on the rest of the family. How many parents when faced with the trials and tribulations in life, instead of dealing with those trials, down a few pills, or simply "run away" for a while? How many of those parents (the teens' supposed role models) take the lead and "teach" their children that the easiest way to deal with their problems is not to rid themselves of the problem, but to simply put a gun to their head and squeeze a trigger? In an instant the problem is gone—and your life of misery is now finished.

How do we teach our young person to be an overcomer when there was no "Overcomer 101" in the classroom? How do you teach a child something that you have no idea how to do yourself?

1 John 1:4, 5
"For whatever is born of God overcomes the world. And this is the victory that has overcome the world; our faith. Who is he who overcomes the world, but he who believes that Jesus is the Son of God?"

I do not believe that anyone sincerely wants to commit suicide. Each person who tries is really crying out for help. They desire to have themselves heard and their feelings understood. This is evidenced by the following powerful words written by teens themselves who have attempted suicide and succeeded by failing.

Here are some of their own words:

"Suicide is not the answer, and whoever tries it needs serious help. Things are better after a while. It's not worth dying. I have lots of reasons to live, and they're better than the stupid reasons to die for."

"Time heals everything."

"Don't keep your feelings in—talk about them with anyone."

"Sometimes you just need a friend to spend time with and to talk to."

"Taking my life solves nothing. If I screw up, like almost failing school, I'll just muddle through and try again. Making some mistakes is definitely not the end of the world."

"Suicide is detrimental and nothing good will come of it. It's a long-term solution to a short-term problem, resulting in long-term grief experiences by close family and friends."

"Suicide is not the answer to anything. Life has its ups and downs, and you need to deal with them and move on."

"While I was in the hospital, my immediate family visited me and I had time to think about if I had succeeded, I would have never gotten to see them again. It was selfish and stupid of me (to have tried to take my life.)"[3]

As the teens themselves have written, suicide accomplishes nothing good. According to the results of an extensive survey conducted by the George H. Gallup International Institute, in cooperation with Blue Cross and Blue Shield, 1,500 teenagers from thirteen to nineteen years old said that friends were the greatest influence among those who thought about, came close to, or tried suicide.

One of the greatest things I learned while reading and studying this subject was the importance of **friends**. I've come to see during the many conversations I've had with teens that they take the word "friendship" much too lightly. I challenge teens continuously to do a study, along with some hard thinking about "true friendship."

I find it interesting that in our society today, with the explosion of gangs, that now, instead of taking one's own life, teens are taking their frustrations out on one another by taking the life of another. I wonder if it truly helps the killer to "feel" like a man?

Our youth are too precious to allow others to teach them how to deal with their situations. Drug abuse, alcohol consumption, and suicide are sweeping like a plague throughout the world. Let us be the ones to teach them the joy of overcoming their problems. The joy that comes through faith in Jesus Christ.

If one falls down, his friend can help him up.
But pity the man who falls and has no one to help him up!
Ecclesiastes 4:10 (NIV)

CHAPTER SIX
WHAT IS A RITE OF PASSAGE?

Before we can look at exactly what the right rite is, we need to have an understanding of what a "rite of passage" is.

In the past seventeen years of ministry to children and youth, I have had the privilege of traveling to more than forty countries around the world. In every society and culture I visited, whether in a first, second, or third-world civilization, I have observed something these many people groups had that was missing from modern Christianity. Though the means by which it was carried out differed from country to country, each one had their special "rite of passage" for their young men and women. A ceremony that is more than a tradition handed down from generation to generation. The "rite of passage" is a way of life, considered to be **the most** important day in a young person's life.

The "rite of passage" is simply this: A "**rite**" is a ceremony, ritual, service or observance that usually comes from the tradition of the people group. I was astounded to find that there are as many different ways to perform these rituals as there are people groups. And there are thousands! One thing I did find, though, was the end result of the ceremony was always the same. Whether it took one hour or one month to complete, the end result was the recognition of the initiate as a man or woman by the entire community from that day forth. The initiate was no longer seen as a child after the event took place. The community as a whole saw and treated the new adult as an adult. His or her peers recognized the new status, and most important was how the new man or woman saw themselves.

The ceremony can sometimes be performed in a few hours. In some cultures the entire process takes place over several months. Along with the ceremony, there is usually a grand celebration that follows. Many times, these celebrations are just as big, if not bigger, than a wedding. In many cases a wedding is part of the service.

A "**passage**," on the other hand, is a voyage or journey. It can be looked upon as a road or channel. Combined with a rite, this "rite of passage" becomes a ceremony or ritual whereby the participant embarks on a journey. In this instance, the journey is one where the child "travels" from childhood, to adolescence, to adulthood. The journey actually begins the day the child is born. This is when I believe the parents' responsibility begins in the "training" of their child.

The planning, preparation, and voyage into adulthood is a long process. If taken lightly by the parent, it will be taken lightly by the child. The more committed the parent is in the preparation of this event, the more seriously the child will look at it. The "rite of passage" ceremony then becomes a celebration of the hard work and efforts of those involved in the process of raising, training, and preparing the child for adulthood. It is truly a joyous occasion where all those involved celebrate to the fullest. It's a day that is never forgotten.

Every teen I've ever ministered to longs for the day when he or she is recognized as an adult. They yearn to be accepted as one who is no longer seen as a child. As they reach the time of puberty, there are things happening to the young person physically, emotionally, and psychologically that scream to be noticed and not ignored. Because of the inadequacies and lack of training on the part of the parents, all too often this crucial time in their life goes unrecognized. The young man or woman is forced to struggle with the changes occurring within alone, or with friends, instead of the ones God created this time to be shared with—the family. As you recognize the child fading and the adult in your child coming to life, this could be one of the most exciting and cherished times in the building of your relationship with your son or daughter.

Your child is at the threshold of the most critical time in his or her life. The decisions you make during this time will affect your child for the rest of his or her life. That old expression "children should be seen and not heard," is a devastating lie that the enemy of our souls wants you to believe and live by.·

For far too long, the enemy has robbed our children of the strong relationships that God has ordained us to have with our children. Your children yearn for you to hear them when they cry out to you (many times with actions more than words). "Hey, Mom, Dad—I'm not a kid anymore!" Be honest. Don't you remember saying (or thinking) those same words when you were a teen?

Have you ever thought about what being an adult really means? Is there a definitive answer for the word "adult"?

Webster's Dictionary says:

1. grown up; mature in age, size, strength, etc.
2. a man or woman who is fully grown up; mature person
3. a person who has reached an age set by law that qualifies
    him for full legal rights, in common law generally twenty-
    one years of age.

After looking at this definition, I thought about what Webster wrote and came to my own conclusions as to what an adult is. What about you? Do you have a personal definition of what being an "adult" is? What does being a man or woman mean to you? Can you think of a specific occurrence that you could say was the "defining" moment when you actually "stepped into adulthood"? When was that time and what were the circumstances that caused it? When was the moment that you knew others recognized you as an adult?

Each one of us has had experiences in our lives that have molded and shaped us into the man or woman we are today. Every one of us at some time in our life longed to be recognized as an adult. At some point in our life it actually happened. When was that "magic moment" for you? Is there really a "magic moment" when all of a sudden you discover the adult within you? When was the time in your own life that you became aware of and sensed others actually relating to you as one who had passed from adolescence into adulthood?

According to what I read in 1 Corinthians 13:11, there actually is a precise time in our lives when something happens to our thought processes. Our demeanor changes, because our own recognition of ourself changes.

1 Corinthians 13:11

"When I was a child, I spoke as a child, I understood as a child, I thought as a child; but **when** I became a man, I put away childish things."

The key word I see here is *when.* When was your when?

Put the book down for a moment and take a few minutes to reflect on that time in your life when you came to the realization that you did "put away childish things."

Go ahead, I'll wait.

Wasn't that refreshing? Perhaps it wasn't. Maybe you were one of those children who was forced to take on the responsibilities of adulthood due to circumstances you had no control over. That's in the past, and with all my heart I pray that you've worked things out in your life, especially in the relationships with those who might have hurt you.

Perhaps you had an abusive parent. Abuse comes in many forms, especially through the eyes of a child—or from one who can't seem to forget a childhood filled with pain. Maybe you were abused physically. Maybe emotionally. Maybe you're mother was forced to be a disciplinarian for lack of a father in the home. Did you have a sibling who always put you down and made you feel worthless? Perhaps your father concentrated the bulk of his time on the job - instead of making it his job to be the father you yearned for him to be. Whatever the case in your life, whatever has caused you to not recognize the adult that you are, I believe it's time to put those things *behind*. It's time to forgive those who have hurt you and *press on* to the future God has waiting for you, not only as His child, but as the man or woman of God He has created you to be.

Not that I have already attained, or am already perfected; but I press on, that I may lay hold of that for which Christ Jesus has also laid hold of me. Brethren, I do not count myself to have apprehended; but one thing I do, forgetting those things which are behind and reaching forward to those things which are ahead, I press toward the goal for the prize of the upward call of God in Christ Jesus. Philippians 3:12-14

"And whenever you stand praying, if you have anything against anyone, forgive him, that your Father in heaven may also forgive you your trespasses. "But if you do not forgive, neither will your Father in heaven forgive your trespasses." Mark 11:25-26

If you've truly done this in your heart, then contact those who have offended you (if possible), and share from your heart with them. Are you married? If so, then share with your spouse and then pray together. Do you attend a church that has a good counseling ministry? Then utilize the resource God has put before you. Share with your Pastor the need you have to receive confirmation from another adult that you truly are a man or woman. When you get that confirmation - then celebrate. The celebration is vital and will be discussed in detail in chapter ten.

Remember this; no matter what you or others think or say about you, you are *"...all the righteousness of God in Jesus Christ."* 2 Corinthians 5:21

Here are a few responses I've compiled from men and women I've interviewed over the years as to when that important step into adulthood took place:

"It happened for me when I got my driver's license. When I saw my picture on that license, it made me feel different. It made me feel older with more responsibility."

"The first time I felt like a man was when I kissed my wife for the first time after we were pronounced husband and wife at our wedding ceremony."

"When I was 14 my dad died. I had to get a job and help with the bills and the care of my brother and sisters. After just a few weeks I felt like a man. Especially when I knew that some of the food on the table was paid for by me."

"When I had my first period. I was 12 years old."

"The first time I really felt like I was a woman was when I found out I was pregnant with my first child."

"It was at the airport, when I said good-bye to my parents and my little sister as I was leaving for college. When I walked down the runway into the plane, I felt more like an adult than ever before."

"The first time I felt like an adult was when I got my first job. When I opened the envelope with my first paycheck and saw my name on it, that was the first time I felt like a man."

The first time I felt like a man was not at my Bar-Mitzvah. The first time I personally felt like a man was the moment I first looked at my daughter, Jeni. It was the first time in my life that I truly felt like a man. I believe it was due to the fact that it was also the first time in my life that I knew I was responsible for the life of another. As I looked at my newborn child, I could see there was no way she could take care of herself. I knew it was my solemn responsibility, so I made a personal vow to do whatever it took to meet her every need.

The ceremony of my Bar Mitzvah gave me a "feeling." The birth of Jeni gave me a "knowing." The ceremony was simply a way of following the traditions of my heritage as a Jew. I was taught to go along with that ceremony.

Wouldn't it have been wonderful to have had that time in your life where you gradually grew into that stage of adulthood with your family and friends celebrating with you? Wouldn't it have been exciting to have your parents publicly bless you as you begin your journey into adulthood with words of encouragement and honor, and then afterward have your parents host a big party in your honor?

THIS CELEBRATION OF ADULTHOOD IS MISSING THROUGHOUT ALL OF CHRISTIANITY

We as Christians do nothing to commemorate and celebrate this most wonderful time in the life of our children. This is something that has been going on for thousands of years throughout all the world, and is still happening today. But why not in Christianity? It is life-changing for those who experience it. When done properly with all the necessary ingredients, it builds character, integrity, discipline, and, most of all, understanding of what being a mature adult in today's world is all about.

After reading the statement, "It takes an entire village to raise a child," thirty-four-year-old Keener Tippin II took the old African Proverb to heart and began the Ujima Academy in Columbia, Missouri. This is a nine-month "rite of passage" program started by Mr. Tippin.[1]

The program is based on tribal African customs when the men in the village would take young boys to an uninhabited place. The boys would explore the land, hunt for food, and eventually find their way home. Some of the lessons they learned embodied the principles of courage, honor, and hope. The older men were teaching the younger the skills necessary to pass from adolescence into manhood.

When the young men returned to the village they were immediately ushered into manhood. Did you get that? Immediately ushered into manhood. There was no second guessing or wondering when the moment would occur. There was a definitive ceremony that took place with a finalization in the recognition of the passage into adulthood.

The modern-day version of the time-honored African tradition encourages youth to stay in school and avoid the snares of crime and drugs.

There are presently an estimated 200-300 "rites of passage" programs in the United States alone. Almost all of these are aimed at keeping the African custom of the "rite of passage" alive in young black males.

In Minneapolis, Minnesota, Chris McNair, a former Methodist pastor, has attracted national attention with the "Simba" program he founded.[2] With the help of adult black men who serve as mentors, Simba teaches what it means to be an African-American male. The three-year program targets boys ages 11-14 and uses a curriculum that addresses issues such as education, career, family, and African American history. After completing an application process that involves both the child and his parents, new members pledge to "learn what it means to be an African American man: spiritually, physically, and socially; to respect myself, others, and God in my conduct and relationships; and to honor my family by applying myself in every situation to achieve my God-given potential." Accused by many as being too "separatist" because the program is for black males, Mr. McNair stresses that he is not teaching attendees to be anti-white, but more of what it means to be black in Christ. Not black "boys" in Christ—but black "men" in Christ!

Some of the others I've found include the Sacramento Rites of Passage Alliance; R.O.P.E. or Rites Of Passage Experience; The Burning Feather; Journey To Womanhood; Muslim Rites of Passage; Pathfinder.

People are discovering the validity of the "rite of passage" experience and are putting it into practice with fantastic results.

One of the overall goals of many of these programs is to provide a system of activities and instruction for African-American youth that prepares them physically, socially, emotionally, intellectually, and culturally for passage into manhood and womanhood.

There are many other Rites of Passage movements that seem to be popping up all over the place. Many of them are secular in nature with a strong emphasis on New Age philosophy. I **do not** recommend these for Christians. A few of them are:

• **EarthSpirit**: a non-profit organization providing services to a nationwide network of Pagans and others following an Earth-centered spiritual path. Based in the Boston area, their membership extends across the United States, and also to several other countries.

• **New Age Voices**: Involved with Astrology, Numerology, Tarot-Reading, I-Ching, Holistic Health & Healing, Self-Transformation and New Age Media.

• **PathFinder**: Rites of Passage are often used to allow anyone access to extraordinary aspects of consciousness. This access brings awareness of what health means for both the individual and the society. An understanding arises which reveals one's own purpose in life as well as that of the culture. This group is now in the Public School System in California!

- **Vision Quest**: "Men's Quest" is a Rite of Passage for men in transition, seeking to find themselves and their higher power. This guided journey allows men to heal themselves as they examine their lives and their relationships. Questing is an ancient and sacred way of making a passage from one life stage to another.

These I just mentioned are but a few. There are many other Rites of Passage experiences that are starting.

It is vitally important for the Christian to be aware of the purpose behind any group that is not affiliated or approved by their church.

What's exciting is to see the many churches here in America, as well as countries around the world where I've spoken and held the *Step Into Adulthood* Seminars, who are beginning to have Rites of Passage ceremonies. In addition, many are instituting mentoring programs for their youth.

There are also many churches who are instituting various forms of the Rite of Passage ceremony as they recognize it's importance, and see the significance to the youth in their congregation.

This is exactly what's been missing in Christianity. It has the potential of changing the future of our churches as we raise, train, nurture and mentor our children to become all that God has for them as future men and women of God. Our children are not the future of our church and society. They are our future **leaders!**

THE BIG DAY ARRIVES

It's the day Ti!Kay has been waiting for.[3] Ti!Kay awakens this day a thirteen-year-old boy. He is a member of the

Kung San (Bushmen) tribe of the Kalahari Desert in Namibia. Today Ti!Kay will leave his village with nothing more than the cloth covering him and his bow and arrow. This day he will shoot his first wildebeest with an arrow. Ti!Kay's father, Kana, and another male adult from the village will help the young hunter track, skin, and butcher the animal. After the meat is brought back to the village, a scarification ceremony takes place (this ceremony is also known as "marking"). This will signify the importance of hunting and Ti!Kay's passage into social manhood. The killing of his first antelope not only provides meat and useful skins and sinews, but in the Kung San village, a young man's successful kill also fulfills a social obligation to his potential father-in-law, who is now provided with meat to distribute to the entire village. He is now considered an acceptable son-in-law by the parents of the girl to whom he has long been betrothed, as his father-in-law now sees that this young man can successfully provide for his daughter.

What I've just shared has been documented by filmmaker John Marshall in a fourteen-minute movie titled *A Rite of Passage* from the San (Ju Wasi) Film Series.

For the youth of the Maasai tribe in East Africa, a different event unfolds. The boy will begin his quest for manhood by giving away all of his childhood possessions. After wrapping himself in a black cloth, he is ready to leave his village. The elders of his particular tribe will then put the boy through an elaborate process of initiation for his passage into adulthood. It is a time of darkness and loss that is then consummated by a hunt. During this hunt, the man-to-be must capture a myriad of feathers from various birds that will be used to make a huge headdress. As a symbol of his rebirth, the youth will wear the bird's nest on his head. Inside the nest grows not only the new hair of the emerging man, but also the dreams and ambitions of adulthood. When the nest is taken off, his head is blessed by elders with water mixed with honey or milk, and then encased in a thick red paint. The hair is then braided into dread-locks, which resemble burning feathers. Red has replaced black and stands for intensity of passion in the young man, passion that is tested and molded through the remaining rituals of his "rite of passage."[4]

In a Melanesian Village in the South Pacific, a young man climbs a sixty-five-foot tower made from bamboo and various other materials. After he gets to the top, he will tie a vine to both ankles. He then takes a leap and plunges to the ground below, stopping only inches from the hard surface. After he settles down, he removes the vines from his now swollen and pained ankles and carefully saunters to where the unmarried village girls delightfully wait. As he nears the young women, his eyes are fixed on the one he's secretly been longing for. He places his hand on her head and they are immediately taken to the village elder who performs the wedding ceremony. The entire village celebrates the boy's "leap" into manhood and the girl's "walk" into womanhood. After the ceremony, both are recognized and accepted as full adult members of the village with all the privileges that go along with being an adult. Then the young husband takes his new wife into the hut he has been building for the past several months in anticipation of this day. And the cycle of life begins again.

Just several hours before these events, these men were looked upon as boys in their respective villages. From now on—they will forever be seen as men.

These are just three examples of what some boys go through to become men. These are three of the easier ways that I've researched. So as not to turn any stomachs upside-down, I've chosen these as the examples. There are as many varied ways that boys become men as there are people groups. Some take a few hours. Other rites take months, where the intended has to do such things as eat raw meat, drink the blood of an animal, go through near starvation and sleep deprivation, go through scarification ceremonies, circumcision and other body piercings that are literally too gruesome to mention. In each case, though, when the initiate is done, he is then looked upon and accepted into his society as a man—with all the privileges that go along with being a man.

There are also various ceremonies involving girls becoming women as well. In some of the tribal ceremonies in the tropical rainforest tribes in Peru, the women are the only ones who have to go through the ceremonies. Some of what they do would cause many men to pass out! But the moment they are completely through their initiation ceremony (which can sometimes be months), they are considered to be a woman—with all the respect and privileges that go along with the title. In these cases it's the new woman who chooses who her husband will be!

THE NEED FOR A MODERN-DAY RITE OF PASSAGE

Today's modern society has lost touch with a basic human need. The need for ritualistic acknowledgment of transition from one stage of life to another. These rites of passage were a crucial part of village life.

Christian teenagers in America and other parts of the world have no clearly marked rituals to make a successful transition to young adulthood. Many parents see their adolescents going through awkward growing pains and identity confusion. They help whenever they can to the best of their abilities, but in many cases it's a cross-your-fingers, hope-for-the-best that the struggling teen will somehow make it into adulthood in today's world. Tribal societies have understood that the transition from child to young adult is so vast that it takes a monumental event to successfully bring about the transformation.

In American society, the rise of gangs and reckless behavior dramatizes the plight of youth who are desperately seeking some sort of initiatory process, in the absence of anything provided by the culture. Ceremonies such as high school graduation have little meaning in today's culture, because the adolescent has not been given tests that truly meet the soul's longing to be engaged in a heroic quest.[5]

Japan was the only country I found that had an entire day devoted to recognizing youth transitioning to adult status. January 15 is a national holiday throughout Japan called "Coming-of-Age Day" or "Seijin-no-hi" honoring all those who have reached their twentieth birthday in the year up to and including this day. In Japan, the age of twenty is regarded as the age when young people attain the responsibility and status of adulthood. They are now legally allowed to smoke, drink, and vote. In cities, towns, and villages all across Japan, there are special celebrations held where the new adults attend dressed in their best. The men usually wear suits and the women come in kimonos called "furisode." There are some who will spend upward of $10,000 in celebration and commemoration of this day.

In some countries, all that's necessary is to catch a bird and bring it back to the village alive. Sound easy? Sometimes it takes the "bird-catcher" days or weeks to capture his prize. American Indian tribes have many different rituals depending on the tribe. One of those rituals involves smoking peyote—a hallucinogenic drug.

Actually, after studying the many varied ways that boys became men, I'm glad all I had to do was memorize a 20-30 minute speech in Hebrew, then recite it to some family and friends along with a few others in the synagogue whom I'd never met before. It took me two years of Hebrew School twice a week, something quite removed from the initiatory rites of other cultures. Some faced the possibility of being some wild animal's lunch, or crashing headfirst into the ground and smashing their skull open in front of all their loved ones! My ceremony or ritual is what most people know as a modern day Bar-Mitzvah.

A DAY I'LL ALWAYS REMEMBER

As a nice Jewish boy growing up in Brooklyn, New York, I was Bar-Mitzvah'd at the age of thirteen. To this day, more than thirty years later, I can still tell you what I had for breakfast, lunch, and dinner, as well as things that occurred from the time I awoke, until I went to bed sometime around 2:30 a.m. It meant that much to me.

Can you tell me any meals you had on any birthday from the age of 12-16? I can. Here's a quick breakdown of the day of my Bar-Mitzvah:

November 13, 1965: I woke up before the sun rose and began some final preparation and study for the most significant day of my life. I was an emotional basket-case. Prior to a breakfast of scrambled eggs, home fries, sausages, orange juice, and an English muffin, I had already showered, combed my hair, and did all the rest of the stuff you usually do in the morning. After eating, I got dressed in a suit and tie. Then, we were off. When we arrived at the synagogue, I was shaking. In about thirty minutes, I would be standing at the front to recite my haf-torah—in Hebrew! This is the Scripture portion I had been going to Hebrew School and studying twice a week for the past two years! Oy vay! I was really scared. After the service, we went home, changed, and my folks said I could have what I wanted for lunch. I chose two cheeseburgers, french fries, and a vanilla coke. Around four that afternoon we left our house for the hall where the party was about to begin! When the party started,

I ate some pigs-in-a-blanket (cocktail franks), knishes, egg rolls, and shrimp. I also had ginger ale and some of the champagne (it's okay, I was now a man). For dinner I had well-done prime rib, a baked potato with butter, hallah (a nice Jewish sweet bread) and carrots. I also had a puff of my first cigar (disgusting) and my first full glass of wine. For dessert I had a piece of "my" cake. We got home about 2:00 in the morning, counted all the "gelt" (money), and went to sleep. That was the day I was Bar-Mitzvah'd! And what a day it was. That was 1965! As of this writing, that was thirty-two years ago!

Nine years later:

October 27, 1974: The day I married Gail. Although it was one of the five most important days of my life, I cannot tell you what I had for any meal that day. I remember our wedding ceremony, some of the happenings during the celebration, and our first night together, but that's all I remember about this wonderful day.

October 17, 1976: I accepted Jesus into my life as my Messiah. I remember seeing the movie *Time To Run* and going into the pastor's office after the invitation, then praying to receive Him. I also remember walking out of the office and seeing the look on Gail's face as I approached her. I don't remember another thing about that day. This was the most important moment in my life.

May 2, 1976: My precious daughter, Jeni, was born. I remember an hour or so prior to her birth, and the moments during and some after. I cannot tell you another thing about that day, even though it was one of the most precious and special moments in my life. The moment I first set eyes on Jeni was without a doubt the first moment I truly felt like a man.

December 15, 1978: Lance was born. As you read in the opening chapter, the unique details surrounding his birth are a true miracle. I was with Gail in the delivery room when Lance came into this world. I remember that moment vividly. I could not tell you another thing about this most exciting and wonderful day in my life.

So why do I remember every detail of November 13, 1965? I believe it was due to the preparation, anticipation, and significance of the day. With my marriage to Gail I had waited for several months. With Jeni, as well as Lance, I waited nine months. For my Bar-Mitzvah, though, I had prepared and studied for years. The anticipation and preparation took place for several years before that special day! I had no idea what being a man was all about, but the adventure was so exciting. I had some idea what marriage was, and also what being a father would be like. But to be recognized as a man after being looked upon as a boy for thirteen years was something I couldn't grasp. When it finally happened I experienced a different feeling within that was truly indescribable! I was a man. Sure I had much to learn, but I would learn these new and wondrous things about life from a different perspective...as a man. **It did not matter to me what anyone else thought.** Because of the laws and traditions of my faith and heritage, I knew deep within that I was looked upon as a man, with all the privileges in the synagogue and our community afforded to men only. I could now be a complete member of the congregation with full rights as an adult.

I saw this same transformation happen in the life of my own son Lance. After the ceremony, you can't help but see yourself differently than before. Not only do you view yourself differently, but your peers see you in a different way as well. Those who haven't gone through any ceremony or recognition look up to you in a way that couldn't be there without the public recognition given during this time. Because other adults now accept you as one of their own, I have found that peers see you differently. I found that adults

who knew Lance and came to his ceremony now spoke to
Lance in a different way than others. The younger children
seemed to look up to Lance with respect. They saw someone they could aspire to be like in a way that was much
more attainable in their eyes than looking at an adult like
me. When they looked at me, it seemed to them that it
would take forever before they would become an adult. But
as they considered Lance, they saw that in just a few years,
they could do the same thing. To the younger child it was a
more attainable goal. But Lance's Bar-Mitzvah was different than mine. Here's why.

What Went Wrong?

As it is in the lives of so many, it was disastrous in my
case. It was also potentially life-threatening. The tradition
was wonderful, the ceremony was thrilling, but the preparation was partial. Now that I was supposedly a man, what
was I supposed to do? How was I supposed to act? If I was
now a man there were things that I should know. Shouldn't
I be able to make decisions on my own? After several months
the thrill was suddenly gone.

Although my parents did what they were taught in keeping with tradition, there was a very important aspect of this
"*passage*" in my life that someone forgot to let me in on.
What was it all about? What was the purpose and long-term
goals? Nobody gave me guidance in the area of manhood.
No one taught me how a man was supposed to behave. It
was all tradition with no meaning instilled. In Hebrew
School I was simply taught to memorize some passages of
Scripture. After all, I had to look good for the people attending. Everything was based on the tradition of my Jewish
heritage. I then surmised (as any man would) that the only
way to be a man was to do what men do. My father smoked,

so I took up smoking at the age of thirteen. Nobody ever taught me what it meant to have good character, reputation, morality, integrity, honor, or destiny. I was never taught anything about goals or goal-planning, or given any direction for my life. At the age of fourteen, I simply began to watch what other men did and copied them. By the age of fifteen I was heavily involved with drugs and drug-dealing, and my life was a disaster. If it weren't for finding my Messiah at the age of twenty-four, I don't know what would've happened to me—but I know it wouldn't have been good.

Train up a child in the way he should go, And when he is old he will not depart from it. (Proverbs 22:6)

I was not trained in the way I should go. I was merely trained as to what I should do for a simple ceremony that lasted all of one hour. I had no idea what I said or what it meant. I was simply taught a speech in another language. I was taught to read that language—not understand it.

Were my parents wrong in the way they raised me and allowed me to be prepared for this service? I don't think so. My parents honored and blessed me by giving me the opportunity to have that ceremony in the first place. They were simply doing the best they could with what they were taught. They gave me as much love as they knew how. One thing that was wrong was the lack of teaching in the things of God, as well as no direction or guidance for the future. The two most important aspects of my life that were needed during my passage into adulthood were IDENTITY and DESTINY. I had neither.

After I married Gail and had children, I decided that my children would be raised differently. What I set out to do was good, but it wasn't right. It didn't get that way until I began to study the Scriptures and put the Word of God to the test in the raising of my children. There are so many varied philosophies on child-raising in the world today that it can leave you desperately confused.

So what is the correct and proper way to raise and train your child? God's way, of course.

**He must know what He's doing, because
He's the only Father who had a perfect Son.**

What greater example could there possibly be?

With Jesus as our example to follow, I saw that He, too, had a "rite of passage." In Luke 3:42, 46, 47 it is written: *"And when Jesus was twelve years old, they went up to Jerusalem according to the custom of the feast...Now it was that after three days they found Him sitting in the midst of the teachers, both listening to them and asking questions. And all who heard Him were astonished at His understanding and answers."*

Jesus spoke in the Temple when He was only twelve years old. This is the youngest age recorded that I've found where a child can have a "rite of passage" and take his first step into adulthood. That's not only true during biblical times when Jesus lived, but it's also true today. You'll also notice that He did it during a time when the greatest feast took place.

Another interesting observation is that *this is the last recorded time in Scripture where we see Jesus as a child.* Finally, I wondered, "Why twelve?" Jesus was Jesus at ten. After some research, I discovered that twelve was the youngest a child could be to speak in the Temple. Prior to that age, you had to be accompanied by a parent. All coincidence? Or is a certain principle being shown to us here? I believe the latter.

CHAPTER SEVEN

LET THE TRAINING BEGIN

A Rite of Passage; Step Into Adulthood; Coming of Age; Bar or Bat-Mitzvah. No matter what you decide to call it, it will be a tremendous opportunity for the individual, the family, and...the extended church family as well. When a family is blessed within the walls of their local church, the pastor has reason to get excited. I believe first and foremost we (as pastors) must ask ourselves at least two questions (and let's be honest about the answers):

- *"What am I doing here?"*
- *"What is my goal for the people in the congregation?"*

From the interviews I've conducted with pastors across America, as well as in many countries around the world, the answer to the first question was pretty standard: *"This is where God called me."* That's as it should be. Why would a pastor choose to be anywhere but in the place he's called to serve? Interestingly, the answer to the second question varied greatly.

- "I want to help *my people* become all that God has created them to be."
- "To feed the Word of God to those I'm called to shepherd."
- "For the congregation to see me as a good shepherd."
- "To build a strong body of believers within the community."
- "Because I wouldn't be happy doing anything else."

- "To be in a place where I can build a strong home-based church family that will touch the world for Jesus."
  (This last one is my personal favorite)

As a pastor who has devoted my personal call to shepherding children and youth, my answer, as it has affected me, is:

- "To be an under-shepherd to the pastor and parents, working together to help the child establish a personal relationship with Jesus; to create a desire for continual growth in that relationship in the following areas:
  - to love the Word of God
  - to respect and honor the family (parents and siblings)
  - to become a functioning, productive adult member of the local, national, and international church body."

What greater gift can we give to families than to assist them in the training of their children? The key word here is assist. In my extensive traveling, I have found that the church today has too often done a great disservice to the family. What the family has done is relegate the responsibility of training their children in matters of Christian growth to the Children's Pastor, Sunday School teacher, and youth pastors.

I hate to disappoint you, but this isn't the way it's supposed to be. As pastors to children and youth, we are an extension of the family. What we should be looked upon to do is to reinforce the teaching and training that the child should already be receiving in the home.

I don't understand how a parent can expect a twenty- or twenty-five-year-old (average age of youth pastors), who has never had children of their own, to teach the child about proper behavior in the home.

I believe this is happening because of ignorance on the part of both parents and pastors. Parents scream, "Help! I've never raised a five-year-old" (or 8, 10, 12, 15, or 17-year-old). So what do they do? They bring them to the church and believe (and hope) that the child will get the right friends. "After all," the parent surmises "since this is the church, all the children and youth who go there are probably Christian and they'll rub off on my children." Not! This is not the mind-set of every parent, but it is with the majority that this veteran children's and youth pastor has seen in seventeen years of ministry in the church.

The pastor, on the other hand, says:

- "Parents are frazzled. I have to un-frazzle them."
- "I'm not 'called' or trained (and have no desire) to work with children."
- "I know! We'll hire a children's pastor! I'll feed the sheep—he'll feed the lambs!"
- "It's the parents' responsibility to train those children, not mine" (even though they have no training in raising a godly child!)"

I've seen and dealt with these types of rationales all too often. This is not the way it's supposed to be—especially in the church. The church should have the resources to help the PARENT raise and train the child according to that old familiar verse, Proverbs 22:6 - *"Train up a child in the way he should go, and when he is old he will not depart from it."*

Here we have the present command and the future promise. Let me paraphrase that verse so as to help better understand what it's saying:

"If we properly train our child today, he will remember it and stick with the faith in the future."

This is where a clear understanding of the words "train up" come in. To train up according to God's Word involves three points:

1. DEDICATION—Our first task is to dedicate the child to God. As we saw in the second chapter, the child is God's creation. The child belongs exclusively to Him. For some reason He chose you as the child's parents or legal guardians for the purpose of the proper stewardship of the child.

2. INSTRUCTION—This is one of the ways this word (train) is used in early Jewish writings. It is the **parent** who is called upon to instruct the child as to what is necessary to cause the child to learn all that is essential in pleasing God.

3. MOTIVATION—A newborn babe sometimes needs its palate stimulated so as to create a desire to take in nourishment. This is the Arabic meaning of "train up." As parents, we too are commanded to create a desire (or taste) within the child so that he or she will be motivated to do what is pleasing to God.

The word "child" refers to the recipient of the training. This word (child) is better translated from the Hebrew by the word **dependent**. As long as the child is dependent on the parents, he is to receive training—regardless of age.

We must also remember the word says to train up a child "in the way **he** should go," not how we think he should go. It is our job as parents to find the strengths of the child and build on those strengths, so as to allow the child to use the giftings God has placed within the child to be used to most effectively bring glory and honor to Him.

Too often, we view our children as an opportunity to correct our personal failures and disappointments in life by trying to fulfill our dreams through them. There's no greater travesty that we can thrust upon our child than this. We must dedicate ourselves to train, motivate, instruct, and inspire our child to become all that God has equipped them to be and do for the glory and honor of His Kingdom—not ours. The greatest illustration of this is found in the words of Joshua:

Joshua 24:15
"...but as for me and my house, we will serve the Lord."

This is where the church can be used to fulfill its call in working together with the parents. There are too many parents who have told me that they have no idea how to creatively and effectively accomplish this in the lives of their children.

The "rite of passage" ceremony within the church is a true vantage point as it is used for the success of training the child as he or she is prepared to take the first steps into adulthood.

Pastors (and parents)—wouldn't it be nice to have young people in the church who have set goals for their future? Where each one looks forward to the day when they are recognized as adults within their church body? Wouldn't it be nice to see them accept some responsibility for the daily and weekly goings-on in the church, instead of just being a pew filler who can hardly wait for the service to end?

In the life of the Jewish child who has a Bar or Bat-Mitzvah, the moment the service is over, the young man or woman is looked upon differently by the entire congregation. This youth is immediately looked upon as an adult member of the fellowship with all the privileges afforded adult members. This includes participating in the various daily and weekly functions, jobs, routines, and responsibilities of the church.

Is this all predicated on one service or ceremony? Not at all. This happens after years of training and preparing the child to not only take a symbolic first step into adulthood, but to also begin accepting the responsibilities that go with the title.

Being a pastor, I wondered what people would think. Most people don't take to change very well. As a father, I had to come to the decision as to what was best not for the church, but for the child. As I prayed and sought the Lord, I always was brought back to a simple question. "What is the goal you have as a pastor?" Being a children's pastor for most of my ministry, I knew that my goal was to help parents be all the parent they were called to be. I was not a substitute parent. There was no way I could possibly instill in any child all I had in my heart to teach them in the two to four hours they were in my care.

It became a desire in my heart to teach parents how to be parents. Thus, the *Stepping Into Adulthood* Seminars have become more than a training session on how to hold a "rite of passage" ceremony. It has become (based on the comments of those who've attended) more of a parenting seminar where parents are shown the awesome responsibility God has given them in training the child He has blessed them with. There is a strong concentration on helping fathers to see the joy of discipling their sons while building a strong relationship in the process. This is also true of father to daughter, mother to son, and mother to daughter relationships.

I believe pastors are called to disciple, train, and nurture those who are part of their fellowship. A big part of this training should be to help parents understand how to parent.

What better way to do this than to institute a program where the parents work along with the church staff in training and preparing their child for a service that involves the entire congregation. Together with the family, the congregation will celebrate as they experience the emergence of those children they've watched grow up, taking their first steps into adulthood.

THE JOURNEY TO ADULTHOOD BEGINS

So when does the training begin? The preparation for this event doesn't begin with your child—it begins with you! You cannot prepare your child for something without first being prepared yourself. When this truth is burned deep within your heart, then I believe the day there is knowledge of a child in the womb is the day the training starts. From the moment you find out there's a child in the womb your actions and attitude will help to mold and shape your child's personality whether you know it or not. Studies have shown that the things you say and do, the way you and your spouse speak to each other, all have a direct influence on the personality of your child. This has been proven through years of medical, biological, and psychological research.

This is something that many people have difficulty in understanding or agreeing with. Whether you agree with this finding or not is irrelevant. Whether you accept this scientific study or not should not make one bit of difference anyway. As a man or woman of God, you should have a strong, loving relationship with your spouse, and there should be excitement over the gift God is about to bless you with—planned or not!

Psalm 127:3
Behold, children are a heritage from the Lord, the fruit of the womb is a reward."
We need to understand our responsibility in taking the greatest care possible of the gift or "reward" God has given us in a way that will honor the giver of the gift. The best way to honor not only the giver, but also the Creator of the gift, is to care for the gift by following the instructions He's given. Those instructions are found in His Word.

The instant your child is out of the womb formal training begins. The moment we take our first breath until the
day we die, we are on a continual journey of learning.

The first thing we learn is how to communicate. We
discover that when we cry, one of several things will happen. Someone in the family (usually Mom) will pick us up
and do one of the following three things:

- Feed us
- Change our messy diapers
- Just hold and cuddle us

The education begins! We then find out that *"goo goo,
gah, gah"* doesn't quite communicate as well as various words
we've been hearing such as *"mama," "papa," "potty."* I think
you get the picture. We then discover how to stop our knees
from hurting due to all that crawling around as we astutely
ascertain, "Why am I the only one crawling around like
this, when everyone else goes a lot faster when they're standing up?" So now you discover how to walk! Now you can
really increase the knowledge level. From the walking stage
you acquire the wisdom necessary to climb up on daddy's
lap; how to chase the dog; open the refrigerator (there's lots
to get at in there); you can now go into your big brother's
bedroom and mess it up; get into Mom's makeup kit; and
on, and on, and on! Just think! You're not even a year old
yet. Wow, there's so much more to master!

So where do we go from here? Kindergarten! Yahoo!
Now we learn how to read and write. Our education con-
tinues each year as we learn about math, science, history,
English, social studies, etc. We graduate from high school
and continue our education in college or trade school. We
might get a job or—who knows— maybe get married and
have our own children.

Can you tell me where in this developing and learning
journey you learned how to be a man or a woman? Do you

remember a particular class on Motherhood 101? Father-hood? Did anyone take a course on how to be a husband? how to be a wife? Where do we learn these things? Actually, we've been learning all along.

We learn how to be a parent from our parents. In coun-seling sessions with many parents I've heard the following:

- *"I hated the way my parents raised me. I'm not raisin' my kids that way!"*
- *"I'm definitely not gonna be the kind of husband that my dad was to my mom."*
- *"My parents were the best. I want to raise my children exactly the way they raised me."*

In each case instruction took place. We learned either how we **want to**, or **don't want to** raise our own children. But which way is the proper way? Only God's way! The instructions He gave us in the Scriptures are the only cor-rect way. God's Words are life. They are truly a *"light unto our paths, and lamps unto our feet."*

If you don't use His Words, you've abused His Words.

WHO IS ACTUALLY TRAINING YOUR CHILD?

If you haven't accepted the responsibility of training your child, I can assure you someone else will. He's the enemy. He is a master at getting your child to believe that you're against him or her, and that the world is for him or her. The enemy will see to it that **someone** will *"train your child in the way he should go"* if you won't accept the re-sponsibility that God has given you. When you don't accept that responsibility, in essence you are giving permission to the enemy to take over.

The enemy will actually use an unaware parent to fulfill his plan for the destruction of a child.

I remember several years ago when a parent came in for counseling with her eight-year-old son, Joey. As I had done with all those I counseled, I first had the parent come in, while the child sat in the reception area. After the usual greeting, I asked the mom what was happening. She took out a bunch of papers, revealing that Joey was failing his third-grade class. All his test scores were in the 40s and 50s. Joey felt like a failure and Mom didn't know what to do to help her son.

I then had the mother wait outside while I spent some time talking to Joey. I knew the parents were in the midst of a separation and going through the process of a divorce. Joey sat on the couch next to me with his head down low. He stared at the floor with this forlorn look on his face. Pretty tough goings for an eight-year-old to have the weight of the world on his shoulders. I'd known Joey since he was born.

After greeting him, I said, "Joey, I'll bet you think you're the reason your parents are separated."

"Uh huh," came the response. "I know I am."

After talking with him as to why that wasn't true, I said something that could only have come through divine revelation. "I see you're one of the smartest kids in your class." At that statement, Joey looked up at me with a look of bewilderment.

"Whaddaya mean, Pastor Jeff? I'm the dumbest kid in my class."

"What makes you say that?" I asked.

"That's what my mom tells me all the time."

Well, I now knew Joey's problem. It was the destructive words coming from the mouth of Mom. To let you know how it all ended, I said, "Joey, tell me the truth. Did you ever study for any of your tests?"

"No," he said.

"See, Joey. I knew it. You are one of the smartest kids in your class."

"How come you keep sayin' that, Pastor Jeff? I failed all my tests."

"I see that, Joey. But let me ask you a question. If you never studied at all for any of the tests you took, and you got about half the questions right, how do you think you would have done if you put some effort into your schoolwork and studied twice as hard?" Picking up the papers his mother had left on my desk, I said, "Let's see. On this test you got a forty-five. If you studied twice as hard, that would probably double your score. What would that be?"

"Ummm—ninety?"

"That's right!"

"How about this test where you got a fifty?"

"Uhhh—a hundred!"

"Yes, Joey—a hundred. Do you see what I mean? You got these scores without studying one second. I want to challenge you to study hard from now on, and you'll see that you're one of the smartest kids in your class, okay?"

"Okay, Pastor Jeff, I'll try."

The next month I received a report from the school principal. The report showed Joey as that month's most improved student.

WHERE DO WE GO FROM HERE?

Over the years I've had many parents come to me with the following question: *"I've really messed up with my child. Is there any way to establish a new relationship?"* I believe so. Your child wants just as much to have a good relationship with you as you do with them. I have yet to meet the child who wakes up in the morning with this thought: "I wonder what I can do today to get my parents really mad at me, and to destroy our relationship even worse than it already is." When you've gone on as many overnight trips with children and teens as I have, you hear them talk about everything (especially if you're the bus driver, and the kids think you can't hear a word they're saying). What I have heard goes more like: "I wish my parents and I got along better. Our relationship stinks." "I wish I could talk with my parents, but they never listen to me." "I'd do anything to have a relationship with my dad, like you do."

If there is a need to reestablish a caring, loving, Christ-centered relationship with your child, then it begins with communication. First, communicate with God in prayer. Pray for Him to restore your relationship. After all, He is the God of restoration and reconciliation. Don't expect it to happen overnight. It may take weeks, months, and in many cases years to build the relationship to where you want it to be. I've been praying for a restoration in the relationship with my older son Brent for about nine years. I'll never stop interceding until the relationship is restored.

COMMUNICATION IS MOTIVATION

When people (especially youth) are **informed**, they're motivated to **perform**. Your child cannot be what you **expect**, until he knows what you **accept**. This can only be accomplished through good lines of communication. The key to a successful relationship (whether with your child, spouse, friends, or co-workers) is to understand how each of you communicates. So often we hear with our ears **what** is being said, instead of **why** it was said. If we could learn this one principle in communication, it would have a great effect on every relationship in our life. The greatest deterrent to a good understanding of communication is **not** recognizing the motivation of the heart.

I heard a story about a young man who was hired as a junior executive for a large company in Dallas, Texas. As was the tradition of the company each Thanksgiving, the senior execs would give the junior execs a turkey for the holiday. The other young executives saw an opportunity to play a practical joke, so they replaced the new man's turkey with one made out of paper maché. The unsuspecting man left the office and hopped on a bus for home. As he was traveling, this single man thought to himself, *What am I gonna do with this huge turkey?* As he was thinking this, a man dressed a bit shabby sat next to him holding a brown paper bag. As they traveled, they began to speak to each other. The young businessman found out that this man with the paper bag just did some general labor to earn enough money for a Thanksgiving meal for his family and four children. Unfortunately, he only had enough to buy some hamburger meat, which is what was in the bag he carried.

"Hey," blurted the young executive. "I have this big turkey here, and I have no use for it. Why don't you take it, mister?"

"I couldn't," said the man.

"I insist, really—please take it," the young exec said.

"All right. I'll take it under one condition. An even trade. You take my hamburger meat, and then I'll take the turkey."

Reluctantly, the young man agreed. When the man got home to his family his excitement overflowed. He called all the children into the kitchen to share the story of the kind-hearted man on the bus who traded him what would have been a hamburger dinner for this poor family for a huge Turkey feast! The children's eyes were wide with wonder as the man opened the box and removed what turned out to be a turkey made of paper-maché. As the eyes of the children went from wonder to sadness, the embarrassed father became visibly upset at the thought of a man doing such a rotten deed to someone in such need. Man's inhumanity to man come alive.

Well, the next day at the office the young executive told everyone how he had the opportunity to do a good deed with the turkey that was provided for him. When the others who played the practical joke on him heard what happened, they were anguishing over what they had done. When they informed the young executive as to what they did, he was downhearted. As soon as work was done he ran to the bus stop and rode the same route to try to find the man who had been the recipient of a harmless, yet what turned out to be a cruel joke intended for another. The young executive's intentions were good. The motivation of his heart was pure. For days, then weeks, the young man tried in vain to find the man who he knew was thinking the worst about him.

So often this same thing happens when we communicate. We cannot understand why the person we're talking with has gotten so upset. Maybe it was with your spouse, one of your children, a friend, or a co-worker that got upset with you for no apparent reason. Then later you found out from another source that something you said or did was taken the wrong way. It happens every day. It will continue to happen until we learn how to communicate properly, with an eye on not what was said, but why.

THE PARENT WHO MADE ME WEEP

As a children's pastor and evangelist, I always got excited when I gave an invitation and a child responded by receiving Jesus. I cannot think of a greater joy in this world than to be used by God as His tool to lead someone into a relationship with His Son. I will never forget a time when there were two children, both about eight years old, who received Jesus together at a church where I was ministering. After the service, I stood in the hallway to see the look on the parents' faces as their children excitedly ran to them to share the good news of what they had just done. The first child ran over to her mom and eagerly tugged at her dress. "Mommy, Mommy, I just asked Jesus into my heart!"

The mother looked sternly down at her daughter and yelled, "How many times have I told you not to interrupt me when I'm talking?"

It was the first time I remember wanting to lash out at a parent vehemently. I didn't. I just stood there watching the spirit of this little girl get crushed by her mother's insensitivity to the child's need at that moment. The little girl was devastated. So was I.

The second little girl then came into view. She, too, saw her mom in the hallway and ran to her, excitedly screaming all the way, "Mommy, Mommy, I did it, I did it! I asked Jesus into my heart in Super Church today! I'm borned again!"

The response from this parent was completely different. The mother politely excused herself from her conversation, knelt down to be face-to-face with her daughter, wrapped her arms around the child, and with tears in her eyes said, "Hallelujah! This is so exciting! Honey, this is what your dad and I have been praying for since the day you were born! Let's go find Daddy and tell him. He's gonna be so excited!"

Both these precious little girls did the same thing that morning. Do you think they both left the church with the same feeling of exhilaration that they should have after making the most important decision of their lives? Do you think they'll both take what they did seriously? What was communicated to these girls from their moms will be etched in their minds for a long time. One with joy, the other with anger and rejection.

When you gain an understanding of HOW you are both communicating, then the relationship can build on a good foundation. Remember, it goes both ways. A good communicator knows how to listen as well as speak.

"But the LORD said to Samuel, "Do not look at his appearance or at the height of his stature, because I have refused him. For the Lord does not see as man sees; for man looks at the outward appearance, **but the LORD looks at the heart.**" (1 Samuel 16:7, emphasis added)

CHAPTER EIGHT

PREPARATION FOR
A RITE OF PASSAGE SERVICE

As I previously mentioned, the training begins at conception. This is both at the conception of the child, as well as the conception in your heart of understanding your responsibilities as a parent.

When I came to understand how important it was for me to give my son Lance a "rite of passage" (in my case a Bar-Mitzvah), I had no idea what to do. Actually, I was even a bit frantic. I called rabbis (I learned the hard way that you don't tell a rabbi you're a Messianic Jew without being prepared for an argument), I went to bookstores, libraries, wrote dozens of letters, and I even went to the Bar-Mitzvahs of people I didn't know so I could learn how to give my son the desire of his heart—a service where he becomes a man.

So many questions swirled in my head. Should I give my son a traditional Bar-Mitzvah? How could I without a rabbi? As I studied the word "rabbi," I came to understand the basic meaning was "teacher of the law." I decided that's what I would become to my son—not only his father, but his rabbi (teacher) as well. We even learned Hebrew together using tapes and books.

I went to synagogues in Phoenix, Albuquerque, and Colorado and set out to find exactly what needed to be done to give my son more than a traditional Bar-Mitzvah. It was my desire to help Lance truly understand what the Bar-Mitzvah was in Jewish tradition. I wanted him to have a full understanding of what the *essence of a "rite of passage"* was, and what it would mean in his life. I could have had a traditional Bar-Mitzvah in a messianic congregation, but I had the desire (as did Lance) to have the service in our local church where I was the children's and youth pastor. This was also the place where friends and fellow brothers and sisters in the Lord were. I also felt it would be a good example for others to see. After fourteen years of ministry to youth at that time, I believed the most important aspect of Lance's *"Step Into Adulthood"* would be to help him fully understand the two most important creeds I could teach him:

HIS IDENTITY **IN** CHRIST   - Who He Is
HIS DESTINY **WITH** CHRIST - Where He's Going

If you can instill these two tenets into the hearts of your children (as well as yourself), you will help them with life principles that will guide them both in the present and future as they continue to build on a firm foundation, which begins by understanding who you are **in** Christ, and where you're going **with** Christ. This is what pastors long to teach to those in their local congregations.

Here are some Scriptures you can use as you guide your child in understanding what every man and woman needs to know. Some of these verses will help you to impart both identity in Christ and destiny with Christ, as many times the two go hand-in-hand:

(Jeremiah 29:11) "For I know the thoughts that I think toward you, says the LORD, thoughts of peace and not of evil, to give you a future and a hope."

(Romans 8:1) "There is therefore now no condemnation to those who are in Christ Jesus, who do not walk according to the flesh, but according to the Spirit."

(Romans 8:2) "For the law of the Spirit of life in Christ Jesus has made me free from the law of sin and death."

(2 Corinthians 5:17, 21) "Therefore, if anyone is in Christ, he is a new creation; old things have passed away; behold, all things have become new. For He made Him who knew no sin to be sin for us, that we might become the righteousness of God in Him."

(Galatians 3:29) "And if you are Christ's, then you are Abraham's seed, and heirs according to the promise."

(Ephesians 1:3-11) "Blessed be the God and Father of our Lord Jesus Christ, who has blessed us with every spiritual blessing in the heavenly places in Christ, just as He chose us in Him before the foundation of the world, that we should be holy and without blame before Him in love, having predestined us to adoption as sons by Jesus Christ to Himself, according to the good pleasure of His will, to the praise of the glory of His grace, by which He has made us accepted in the Beloved. In Him we have redemption through His blood, the forgiveness of sins, according to the riches of His grace which He made to abound toward us in all wisdom and prudence, having made known to us the mystery of His will, according to His good pleasure which He purposed in Himself, that in the dispensation of the fullness of the times He might gather together in one all things in Christ, both which are in heaven and which are on earth; in Him. In Him also we have obtained an inheritance, being predestined according to the purpose of Him who works all things according to the counsel of His will."

(2 Timothy 1:9; 2:1) "Who has saved us and called us with a holy calling, not according to our works, but according to His own purpose and grace which was given to us in Christ Jesus before time began....You therefore, my son, be strong in the grace that is in Christ Jesus."

(Acts 26:18) "To open their eyes, in order to turn them from darkness to light, and from the power of Satan to God, that they may receive forgiveness of sins and an inheritance among those who are sanctified by faith in Me."

(Romans 8:28-31) "And we know that all things work together for good to those who love God, to those who are the called according to His purpose. For whom He foreknew, He also predestined to be conformed to the image of His Son, that He might be the firstborn among many brethren. Moreover whom He predestined, these He also called; whom He called, these He also justified; and whom He justified, these He also glorified. What then shall we say to these things? If God is for us, who can be against us?"

(1 Corinthians 6:11) "And such were some of you. But you were washed, but you were sanctified, but you were justified in the name of the Lord Jesus and by the Spirit of our God."

(Galatians 2:20) "I have been crucified with Christ; it is no longer I who live, but Christ lives in me; and the life which I now live in the flesh I live by faith in the Son of God, who loved me and gave Himself for me."

(Philippians 3:13-14) "Brethren, I do not count myself to have apprehended; but one thing I do, forgetting those things which are behind and reaching forward to those things which are ahead, I press toward the goal for the prize of the upward call of God in Christ Jesus."

(2 Timothy 2:21) "Therefore if anyone cleanses himself from the latter, he will be a vessel for honor, sanctified and useful for the Master, prepared for every good work."

(1 Peter 5:6-9) "Therefore humble yourselves under the mighty hand of God, that He may exalt you in due time, casting all your care upon Him, for He cares for you. Be sober, be vigilant; because your adversary the devil walks about like a roaring lion, seeking whom he may devour. Resist him, steadfast in the faith, knowing that the same sufferings are experienced by your brotherhood in the world."

There are many more scriptures that deal with one's identity and destiny. Pastor Wendell Smith put together beautiful study cards on several subjects. One of those subjects is *Identity in Christ*. You can order one by calling this number: 1-800-304-CITY and ask for information on The Rhema Card. You can also write them for information at:

> The Rhema Card
> 15015 Main Street
> Suite 200
> Bellevue, WA 98007 USA

Many people have asked me: "When's the right time for my child to have this ceremony?" "What kind of service should I have?" "Where should I have it?"

So where do you begin? You've already begun. By reading this book you have shown that you see the significance and have the desire to do something about helping your child *"Step Into Adulthood."* The next step is to pray. Ask the Lord to guide and direct you as you seek to bless your child. If your child is at an appropriate age, sit down **with the child,** and discuss what you want to do with regard to a service. Make sure he or she understands **WHY** you want to do this. This is not for your benefit—it's to bless and honor your child. **Let them know this.** Search for appropriate resources for your child's age. I have a list of good resources for training and discipleship in the back of the book.

MY DAUGHTER AND THE RITE OF PASSAGE

When Jeni was fifteen years old, she came to me and announced that she wanted to go to Africa with Teen Missions. She actually had wanted to go to Africa since she was twelve. Teen Missions is an international missions organization devoted to sending teenagers around the world. They have been doing it for years and have sent more than 25,000 teens to every continent on the earth. When Jeni first came to me with this idea I was a bit taken aback. I thought, *Where did she ever come up with this idea?* My wife, Gail, reminded me that she got the idea from her dad. (That's right—me!) She had heard all the stories from me about the mission field and her desire to get involved in world missions continued to grow.

Instead of going to Africa that year, Jeni decided to go to Australia. To send Jeni to the other side of the earth for two months was very difficult. But as I watched her prepare and raise the more than $3,000 dollars needed for the trip, I saw her blossoming into a wonderful young woman of God. She knew who she was (identity), and where she was going (destiny).

I'll always remember the night before she left for her training camp in Merritt Island, Florida. We took a walk together on a clear, warm, star-filled summer night. As we walked, we held hands and spoke about her adventure that would begin the next day. It was a beautiful time. At one point, I affirmed to her how proud I was to be her father, and how much I saw my "little girl" growing into a mature, responsible young woman of God. As I gave her my blessing, I wept as I looked into her eyes and told her that what she was doing was good. There was no fanfare, no music, no big party. I was simply a father filled with pride and love for his daughter—wanting the best for her—and releasing her to follow the call in her life.

I believe Jeni's "Step Into Adulthood" took place that night.

Two years later, Jeni finally went to Africa. The following year after that, she moved there to go to Bible School and work with Zulu children. Her childhood dream since she was twelve had finally come true.

SUGGESTED ACTIVITIES AND RITES OF PASSAGE SERVICES

There is no absolute when it comes to planning and preparing a "rite of passage" service. I wish it were that simple. But here-in lies the beauty of this event. Here is an opportunity for the parent to plan one of the most significant events in the life of their child. This can be done by the parents alone, or if you prefer, with the help of the child. Within the confines of the local church, I would suggest putting together a team of men who work together in the planning of what will be done to help recognize the passing into manhood for boys, as well as a group of women who would do the same for girls being recognized as a woman.

You can establish informative seminars for parents (I would personally recommend my *Stepping Into Adulthood* Seminar). You can then begin to plan educational seminars for the youth who will be in training, along with educational programs, field trips, mentoring programs, challenge courses, or short-term missions trips (my personal favorite). This can be a tremendous time of planning together. I am sure there will be alterations, modifications, and revisions in what's decided and done as each group sees what is working most effectively within their respective programs.

Here's a general guide to use when planning for your "Rite of Passage" or "Step Into Adulthood" program:

Define your goals
The main goal is to design a plan of study where the young person is taught to understand what it means to be a man or woman in today's society. I see this as a two-step process. What are some of the characteristics that you believe need to be imparted into the life of your child?

<u>*In Family/Marriage Relationships:*</u>
- Trust
- Love

- Honor
- Faithfulness
- Commitment
- Parenting Skills

Moral Character:
- Integrity
- Honesty
- Fairness
- Good Work Ethic
- Courage

In the Church:
- Commitment
- Tithing
- Moral Integrity
- Support of the Pastor/Staff
- Giftings

Where does one learn these principles? Do we have to wait until we're grown to be aware of responsibility as adults in today's world?

Preparation Time

This is the time when you'll be preparing the child for the ceremony. The length is up to you. Here's where planning skills come in handy. If this is going to be done through the church, then I would recommend speaking to the pastor and putting together a group who would be willing to work out a specific program that would best suit your particular church format. Remember, there are no absolutes here. You are introducing a new program to the church body, and a little room for testing what works best for you is necessary.

Here are two options:

1. Design and implement a program on your own.

2. Put together a team of other interested adults in designing a program. You can include youth on this team.

PUT TOGETHER A RITE OF PASSAGE EXPERIENCE (ROPE) OR STEP INTO ADULTHOOD (SIA) PLANNING TEAM.

Actually the name is not important as long as you achieve the end result you're looking for. Have the team come up with several different programs for implementation within your church. Remember it is not necessary for this service to be done in the church. If you have a pastor who is not too keen on the idea of taking church time for this, there is nothing to stop you from having a ceremony in your own home. The important element is that your child is trained and recognized as the adult he or she is becoming. I personally doubt a pastor would turn down an opportunity to have the church body participate in a service where the youth of the church will be blessed and honored because of their commitment in becoming more mature men and women of God. The positive effect this service will have on the church body will be cause enough for any pastor to give his whole-hearted blessing. As a matter of fact, I believe that most pastors will look forward to being a part of the planning team.

Some Things for Your Team to Discuss:

• A curriculum for training the child in understanding what being a man or woman is all about (there are materials for suggested reading in the back of the book)

• The length of time for study and preparation

- Qualifications and criteria for beginning the program in regards to the age and maturity level of the child
- Type of service or ceremony
- Frequency of a service: once a month, quarterly, or once a year.
- Involvement of parents (very important!)

The Responsibilities That Are Expected of an Adult in the Following Areas Should Be Taught
- Spiritually
- Socially
- Emotionally
- Intellectually
- Culturally

Remember these models are nothing more than guidelines to help you develop your own program.

As I've stated so many times in my *Step Into Adulthood* Seminars: "It's not important **"what"** you do, it's important **"that"** you do. You'll be both surprised and blessed when you see that as you plan and work together with a planning team or simply you and your child, that your relationships will grow as you plan one of the most significant events in the life of your child.

CHAPTER NINE

THE RIGHT RITE

So what do you do when there is no tradition to follow? Can I simply take my child on a Safari to Africa and let him hunt for a lion? How about if I let him climb to the top of a telephone pole and take a flying leap with a rope tied around his ankles? Better yet, I'll send him into the ocean and let him bring me a shark's tooth. There are so many different ways that are used for youth to step into adulthood that there are volumes of books on that subject alone.

QUESTIONS! OY VAY, DO I GET QUESTIONS!

Traveling to different parts of the world and introducing this concept for the first time in various places causes many people to take notice of its importance and significance. As a result, I am bombarded with questions regarding the details of what could be done to institute a service or ceremony of this nature within the church. Following is just a sample of some of the questions I get asked:

* What if we want to have a Bar-Mitzvah, based on the Jewish rite of passage?
* Can you have a Bar-Mitzvah if you're not Jewish?
* What, actually, is the right age for a ceremony?
* What kind of ceremony can or should we have?
* How do we show our child that we recognize he or she has reached "the age" necessary to have a service?
* Is age really that important?
* Does age have any significance?

- If I do nothing, will it affect my child?
- How big a ceremony do I have to have?
- Where can I have this ceremony?
- Do we do it in the church?
- Do we have it in our home?
- Do we rent a hall?

It goes on and on! As a Jewish believer, of course I would personally love to see the traditions of the Jews brought into the church. Having a Bar or Bat-Mitzvah ceremony as part of the service every so often would be wonderful. After being a part of the Christian community for more than twenty years now, I've come to see that this would be very difficult, since the "order of service" in a traditional church is so far removed from that of a typical Saturday service in the synagogue. As a Jew it's exciting to see so many Messianic churches being raised up around the world.

Now, please understand me. I am not saying that what we need is a typical Bar-Mitzvah as the "rite of passage" ceremony for your child. What I am saying is that you need to do something—anything to help your child celebrate the passing from adolescence to adulthood.

TRADITION, TRADITION!

This is how a tradition begins. A tradition of this kind begins when one is convicted of the fact that something needs to be done for their child. As you see what a blessing this new "tradition" is to your own children, you'll have a desire to see your child continue the tradition with their own children as well. As the years pass, so does the tradition—to our children's children and their children and on and on for generations to come.

The "tradition" of blessing children started in the Book of Genesis with Abraham. In Genesis 18:19 the Abrahamic Covenant was based on Abraham's willingness to train his children. What greater way to bless your child than to teach him about God? This has been going on for thousands of years. There have been "rites of passage" since the beginning of man. The spoken blessing is an integral part of the "rite of passage" ceremony. The spoken blessing touches the heart, soul, and spirit of the one receiving the blessing. A spoken blessing also communicates to the child in an audible way that they're cared for. It's difficult for a child to think they're not cared for, when continual blessings are spoken over them (audibly) on a daily, weekly, or monthly basis. As a matter of fact, this is also true if the spoken blessing is only done once in a lifetime!

In *The Blessing*, authors Gary Smalley and John Trent write of the five key elements of the blessing.[1] These are:

1. Meaningful touch
2. Spoken words
3. Expressing high value
4. Picturing a special future
5. Active commitment

God used the "spoken word" to bless His children from the first of creation. He gave verbal blessings to Adam and Eve (Genesis 1:28); Abraham (Genesis 12:1-3), and Jacob (Genesis 32:24-32). If our heavenly Father sees fit to verbally bless, how much more should we be doing the same for our children.

In chapter 27 of Genesis, before Isaac blessed Jacob, Jacob was instructed by his mother, Rebekah, to go and get his father's favorite foods. Rebekah was going to prepare a meal for the "celebration" of Isaac blessing their son. You see blessings, passages, and celebration all throughout the Scriptures, especially relating to children and youth!

In Deuteronomy 6:1-9, the Israelites were given specific instructions to train their children in the ways of God. They were promised a threefold reward for their obedience: (1) Long-life, (2) Things would go well for them, and (3) Their nation would increase mightily.

SOME RITES ARE WRONG

Actually, there are many *"rites"* that happen on a daily basis here in the U.S. that we're not even aware of, or recognize as *"passages."* There's a vital element missing in each of them.

THE HUNTER

There are literally tens of thousands of hunters in America today. There's a "ritual" that takes place annually in the lives of many of these hunters. For years a father takes his son hunting with him. With each passing year, the son yearns for the day his dad recognizes his manhood. Traditionally, somewhere around a boy's twelfth or thirteenth birthday, his dad hands him his first rifle. Sometimes it's brand new. Other times it may be the rifle that was given to the father by his father. This is usually done only after there's been years of training as to the proper use and care of this potentially life-threatening weapon. The day finally arrives. As the father and son prepare to embark on another of what has become an annual journey (remember, one of the meanings of "passage" is "journey"), the father will be giving a gift of more than a piece of metal. He'll show his son that he has trust in his decision-making ability and that he's reached a level of maturity that warrants a reward.

Along with this passage comes an awesome responsibility. The boy is looked upon by his father as one who can handle a weapon that has the potential of taking a life. From the hunters I've seen and interviewed, this is not taken lightly. For more than 90 percent of those I spoke to and observed, this is a very special moment. The father truly is entrusting his son with a huge responsibility. There is usually some "ceremony" involved. It is most times private—between father and son—and at other times involves the entire family. The "ceremonial closure" takes place when they bring home the "fatted calf" (or in most cases the deer). As the rifle passes from father to son, an important "passage" takes place.

So what's missing here? From what I've witnessed (based again on personal observation and interviews), in almost every case, the following lessons are "taught" to the boy.

- Proper handling, care and maintenance of a weapon.
- Safety procedures when hunting (most states require a hunter safety certificate).
- How to hunt for the intended prize (birds, small and large game).
- How to clean and care for the "kill."
- How to cook your meals outdoors.

All of the above is wonderful. The father teaching his son these skills is doing a fantastic job of training his child how to hunt responsibly. The time spent together is time that creates great memories as well as building on the father/son relationship. But what about manhood? Teaching a boy to be a great hunter does not mean he will be a great or good man. There are significant and vital lessons that need to be taught: integrity, purpose, moral character, husband/wife relationships are just a few.

Now don't get me wrong all you hunters and NRA Members. You are doing more than many men by spending this time with your child. (I didn't say boy here, because of the fact that this qualifies as something you can do with either your son or daughter.) But let me ask you a question here. *Is this quality time?* Are you spending time with your child **AFTER THE HUNT?** The hunting trip is usually one week a year. What do you do with your child after the hunting trip has become a memory? Did you truly use this time to input qualities into your child that will help him or her to become a mature, responsible adult? Or has your child learned that going hunting with Dad is more of an opportunity to carry Dad's bags and get berated any time something isn't right? Does your son or daughter still look forward to those hunting trips? Or do they look for ways to get out of going? Only you know the answer.

What are you teaching your child about becoming an adult, Mr. Hunter? Teaching your child about the joy of hunting is wonderful. With all my heart I wish it were something my own dad did with me. Is your main goal to have a trophy for the wall? That's what most hunters tell me. Yes, in big-game hunting they want to "get the kill" and have some meat for the freezer. But each hunter I spoke with said they would love a "trophy." In your zeal for this trophy, don't kill the desire in your child's heart to spend quality time with you.

You can concentrate on your hunt for a prize to value, or you can use this time to build values in a prize you already possess—your child.

PUBERTY

Ted's a fifteen-year-old high school student. This is his year to reach puberty. Hair is growing all over his body. With puberty comes a change in his outlook on everything. Ted's been eyeing Kate. Kate's been a classmate of Ted's since third grade. He never really thought much about her. She was just another girl in the same class. During the summer, Ted saw Kate at the grocery store and other places in town, and began to notice her in a different light. When he looks at her now, something happens that's never happened before. This same girl who he looked at just a year ago with thoughts of ugh have now turned to thoughts of hug!

All the other guys (whether they're honest or not) tease Ted about his virginity. He gets up the nerve to ask Kate out to a movie. After the movie they talk quite a bit and find out many things about each other. Apparently, Kate has had a crush on Ted since last year. She has "feelings" for Ted that he was unaware of, until today—and as a result they click. So do their hormones. In the heat of the moment, virginity is given up that night. The young man "conquers" his first girl, and a "passage" takes place that night—for both of them.

Possessing the desire and ability to have sex absolutely does _not_ make a boy into a man. The ability to bear children does _not_ make a girl a woman.

GANGS

Mike is a fourteen-year-old boy who has problems at home. His father left before he was born and he never felt like he "fit in" with the rest of his family. He has no sense of what a family is. He has two older sisters who are trying to go to school and be mom to the rest of the family because Mike's mom has to work two jobs. A local gang has a group of "brothers" who are always looking for new "family" members. They won't hassle you; they'll let you smoke, do drugs, supply you with girls—whatever it takes to keep you happy and devoted. To be a member of this family all you have to do is help rob a liquor store. Do this one thing and you're in. Your big night comes. You do the deed with some help from your friends and it's done. You're now a member of the "family." Your new brothers are committed to you—as long as you stay committed to them and the rest of the family.

Two years have passed and you're sixteen now. You've been a vital part of the family for a few years now. So you get more responsibilities—with more rewards for taking them. Someone's been messing with one of the family sisters. It's your turn to teach your family's enemy a lesson. It's time for your first "kill." Do the deed, and there's total allegiance to you because of your allegiance to the "family." A life is taken as a passage takes place tonight.

The next "hit" is from a rival gang. This time you're the target.

COLLEGE BOUND

Your child has never been away from home for more than a couple of weeks to summer camp. Your son or daughter just graduated from high school and has been accepted to a college 800 miles from home. He'll be on his own for the first time in his life. You celebrate with a going-away party. The day he leaves a passage takes place.

MENARCHE

Eighth grade ends and you leave with your family for summer vacation. Sometime during those two months menarche takes place, and all of a sudden your daughter's body begins to develop. You and your daughter have to purchase items at the store she never had to buy before. You have to take her shopping for her first sanitary napkins and her first bra. When she goes back to school, she's a bit uncomfortable because she knows that something has changed and everyone is looking at her differently (especially boys), and another passage takes place.

In some of the passages mentioned (except possibly in the case of the rifle and college), there are some vital elements missing. An understanding and explanation of what is happening; blessing by an adult; a recognition by others with a public proclamation, and a celebration. Also, if each one of the people mentioned was not ***properly prepared*** for their passage, the results could be disastrous. In the cases mentioned there's the potential for the following: runaways, stress, suicide, STDs (sexually transmitted disease), death, pregnancy, abortion, prison.

THE NEED FROM WITHIN

There is such a deep-seeded need to have a "rite of passage" that the youth of today are creating their own. To give an example, body piercing is a form of primitive tribal initiations that have been going on for generations. This is what is considered to be a "barbaric rite of passage." Suicide would fit in this category as well. Life-threatening activities such as Bungee-jumping would be another form of a self-seeking "rite of passage."

THE RIGHT RITE FOR YOUR CHILD

In his book *Men From the Boys*, Professor Ray Raphael from the University of Nebraska has some tremendous insight and helps to confirm what I've found over the years. He points out that the old style rites of passage helped to give the participant a clear identity and sense of self-worth with a keen understanding of his adult role in society. On the other hand, he shows how modern-day rites of passage (as mentioned) do not work. He shows how many adults (especially males) in their twenties and thirties are caught in an "extended adolescence." He also confirms my findings when he shares how many of today's youth are creating their own rites of passage and are unsure as to whether they've passed the test. This is due to a lack of confirmation. Because there is no "**ceremonial closure**," the test of manhood needs to be proven again and again.

He points out how in primitive societies everybody passed the test. There were never any males wandering around the tribe who failed. When you compare today's modern rites of passage, you see that many of our rites are competitive, and for each group of winners, there are always losers. Guys that failed to make the team; gals who didn't make the cheerleading squad; failing a test; flunking out of school; not getting a date. All of these are things that can be devastating in a persons life.

THE PROPER PASSAGE

For a proper passage from adolescence to adulthood to take place, with all the benefits for the young person, there needs to be proper training, planning and preparation. You need to come to an understanding with your child on exactly what it is you are looking to accomplish with the ceremony. Of course you want to have this be a blessing for the child, but what exactly are you wanting to achieve? What is the end result you are looking for?

As I mentioned before, there are two areas that I believe need to be stressed: identity and destiny. These two are important areas that need to be instilled in the life of the child. At what age is this accomplished? It can be thirteen for one and seventeen for another. Each child is different and matures at different levels, depending on so many different things such as: parental training, friends, education, media exposure, etc. When there is a complete understanding on both ends (yours and the child's) of what their identity in Christ is all about, as well as an understanding of their destiny or purpose in life, then you can begin to plan a ceremony where the child will be recognized and blessed publicly.

LANCE'S "PASSAGE" INTO ADULTHOOD WAS NOT AT HIS BAR MITZVAH!

On March 31, 1992, Lance taught me and nine others a lesson in integrity. I had put together a fund-raiser for our ministry, Joy International, called "The Snuggles & Friends 101 Mile Death Valley Walk." The purpose of the walk was to get sponsors for so much per mile to raise funds for our children's home in India. The walk was grueling! The first day of the walk I made the horrible mistake of walking the first several miles in my oversized clown shoes. That proved to be a very bad idea. On the fourth day of our five-day walk, at the seventy-sixth mile, I could walk no more. I actually could not take one more step. The blisters on four of my toes were so bad that it was difficult for any of the team members to look at them. I sat in the support vehicle and wept.

Lance, along with two children's pastors from Colorado who had joined me in the walk, had already walked two miles farther from where I stopped. The motor home picked them up and brought them back to where I was waiting.

When they arrived, you could see the look of concern on Lance's face. When I had announced that I couldn't walk anymore, Lance spoke up. "Dad, from this point on, I'm gonna walk for you." It was a noble gesture coming from a thirteen-year-old. I was doing the walk as Snuggles, (my clown character). I decided to have a small ceremony as I took off my big red round clown nose and placed it around the neck of my son. I then gave him my hat and prayed with the team. After praying, I instructed the driver to take Lance two miles back up the road to where he had left off. When he said no and that he would walk from where we were, I said, "But, Lance, you already walked these two miles." The true meaning of integrity was taught to me (as well as our entire team) that day.

Lance looked me in the eye and said, "That's right, Dad. But when I walked those miles, I walked them for me. I'm not walking for me anymore. I'm walking for you, and you didn't walk those miles yet."

As I sat in the support vehicle and watched my son walk out into the desert I began to weep. I did not see the little boy who walked the last seventy-six miles, but the young man who was walking the next twenty-five.

It was just a few months later that we had Lance's formal Bar-Mitzvah ceremony and celebration.

WHAT KIND OF CEREMONY IS NECESSARY?

The kind of ceremony you have is totally up to you. After all, this is a "new" tradition for all. Does it need to be public? I think so. During my research I never found a "rite of passage" that wasn't. The emerging out of adolescence into adulthood that your child is experiencing is something wonderful. If you are beginning to recognize the "adult" in your child's life, then you should want to share (as well as announce it) with others. Throughout history, in almost every case of the "rite of passage," the ceremony would take place in the village or community where the child is best known. This was a time for everyone in the celebrant's circle of friends, relatives and all those who knew the child to celebrate together this most wonderful time in the young person's life. That time was considered the most important and significant event in the life of the child.

WHAT'S A PARENT (AND PASTOR) TO DO?

In the case of today's ceremony, the reason for having it in the church is usually because, in most cases, many of the child's friends are there, as well as your friends, to share in what is a sincerely joyous occasion. The church today has taken the place of the small villages and communities of yesteryear. I find it very interesting that in the modern church today, there is a "movement" all over the world that is bringing the church into the homes in what has become known as the "Cell Church Movement." This movement is focusing on building intimate relationships in a small community or family setting. I find this to be an ideal setting for the celebration of the stepping into adulthood ceremony, where the church might be too large in numbers. I have seen youth groups around the world that number into the hundreds. Such a large group could become a problem for the pastor to arrange schedules for the ceremony portion of the "rite of passage."

Obviously, the details would have to be worked out in each case with the pastor of your church. I do not know of many (or any) churches doing anything like this, so it will be something unique that you are presenting to the pastor. As you share what your intentions are, I would find it hard to believe that your request would be denied. I cannot imagine a pastor turning down a parent's request to publicly bless their child and to help the child take their first steps into adulthood.

If you're a part of a large congregation where this idea is catching on, and the "Step Into Adulthood" ceremony is beginning to take up too much time, and you're not attending a church with a cell or home-group format, then here's what I recommend. Use the facility at a different time. You could speak to the pastor about using the church on a Friday or Saturday evening, or even Saturday morning. You could then send out invitations to all your friends and relatives and have a service. There are no set rules here. Remember, the important matter here is not when you have it or where you have it. The most important aspect of the whole idea of the "rite of passage" is THAT you have it!

THE CEREMONY

Putting together a ceremony to bless and honor your child can be a scary thought, especially when it has so much significance. First, you need to sit down with your child and allow him or her to be a part of the planning. I believe this is vital. This is not the time for a surprise party. This is very important to your child and has incredible meaning and purpose in the growth and character development of your child. I believe it is absolutely essential for them to be a part of the planning of the event. As you all fully understand why you're doing this, it becomes easier to plan. You are, in essence, sharing with the community that your child is becoming an adult. The child is now ready to begin accepting more of the responsibilities for their actions and life, and this is something you want to share with your family and friends.

I recommend that you allow the child to share some favorite Scripture, and what that Scripture means in his or her life. Perhaps your son sings. Allow him to share a song that has had meaning in his life, or have a friend who sings do a special song in honor of the "new adult." I attended Naomi Porter's Bat-Mitzvah (a girl's passage, where I was invited to be the "rabbi" so to speak). Naomi did a special dance to the Lord that she personally choreographed. As I watched her "dance unto the Lord," it brought me to tears as I literally saw this precious young woman publicly share and celebrate her love for the Lord.

I also saw where a parent allowed friends and relatives to individually come forward and speak words of public blessing to their son. Each person shared for a minute or two what their relationship with the "celebrant" has meant; how their lives were touched; some humorous stories; and simple words of love and blessing to the celebrant.

One of the most important aspects of this time is the public recognition by the parents, with some form of declaration spoken in the blessing where the parent is showing that a true "passage" is taking place.

As you can see, there's no set way to do this. It takes prayer and planning. Working together as a family is all part of the excitement and joy of this experience. Remember, this is the ceremony. The celebration is yet to come. When properly planned, it's a party that is truly remembered.

CHAPTER TEN

LET'S CELEBRATE

In EVERY example I found where a *"rite of passage"* takes place, it was always followed with a celebration. Many times the two would happen simultaneously. From what I could see, these celebrations were often bigger than a wedding ceremony, and again there were times when the wedding ceremony was a part of the "rite of passage." It showed me the significance and importance of this event. This was no small deal.

From what I could find, the occasion was a time for the mother to really shine. After all, she had quite a bit to do with the nurturing and upbringing of the child as well. Although in most cases it was the father who did the preparing of the child for the **ceremony**, it usually was the mother who planned the **celebration**.

Is a Party Really Necessary?

Can you imagine a wedding, where after all the solemnness of the ceremony, the father of the bride says, "That's all folks, thanks for coming?" I don't think so! Why the celebration after the ceremony? How about the big game on Friday night. You're on the high school basketball team and your school is playing for the state championship. The final seconds tick off the clock and your team wins! After the game, the coach thanks everybody for the year's success and says, "Thanks for comin' out and bein' a part of our championship team. Now go home. I'll see y'all next year." I don't think so! Having something so wonderful to celebrate without a big bash of a party would be like going to a dance with no music. It just wouldn't be the same.

We live in a celebration society! Think of all the things we celebrate; birthdays, anniversaries, graduation from elementary school, junior high, senior high, college, a new job, the 4th of July, the New Year, Christmas, Thanksgiving, St. Patrick's Day, Groundhog Day! You get the picture. Well, if we put in the time, energy, and effort to celebrate things that mean so little, how much more planning and celebrating should be done for when our child takes the first steps into adulthood! When they choose to follow the teaching and admonition of their parents, and they recognize and accept the responsibility that goes along with being called an adult—isn't that time to celebrate?

When there's something to celebrate, then celebrate! What better reason could you have to throw a party than to share the joy of this major milestone in the life of your child?

PARTYQUETTE

There really is no specific party etiquette (or partyquette as I call it) that I know of. I've been to Bar-Mitzvahs where the parents spent literally tens of thousands of dollars to celebrate with friends and family. You're simply limited by your availability of funds—and a good imagination with proper planning. But I wouldn't know all that much about it, because it was my wonderful wife, Gail who planned the bash for Lance. And it was fantastic.

Don't let the party itself overtake the purpose for the party.

Let people know why you're doing what you're doing. As those attending come to an understanding of the significance of what's taking place, it becomes a starting point for them to begin the planning and preparation for their own children.

In too many Jewish homes, the Bar-Mitzvah has become a mere tradition. You do it because it's expected. As I mentioned in a previous chapter, tradition without purpose is worthless. There's been too much emphasis on the celebration instead of the celebrant. The "what" instead of the "why."

Here is an excerpt of a sermon titled: In Defense of the Bar/Bat Mitzvah given May 24, 1996, by Rabbi Barry H. Block:

> One Saturday morning, when I was serving a congregation in the Chicago suburbs, I walked into the sanctuary where a Bar Mitzvah was about to take place. To my surprise, all the men in the room were wearing bright red yarmulkes, which looked very much like the head coverings worn by Catholic Cardinals. Another rabbi remarked that it looked like the pope's birthday. Later, when we went into the auditorium, we saw on each table a tremendous center-piece consisting of a basketball goal, several feet high off each table, featuring the logo of the Chicago Bulls. Now, we understood the reason for the bright red kipot. This Bar Mitzvah, like many at that congregation, had a theme. The theme was the Chicago Bulls, whose team color is bright red.
>
> People who know me are aware that I am emphatically not a fan of the Chicago Bulls. However, that was not the reason for my revulsion at the Bar Mitzvah theme. My complaint, instead, was that the emphasis for this life cycle event had been turned away from the religious meaning of

the occasion, away from a young man's acceptance of the Torah, and toward his adoration of a professional basketball team. From time to time, even greater material excesses associated with a Bar or Bat Mitzvah have hit the national press. Who can forget the Bar Mitzvah party held in the Orange Bowl, complete with elephants, or the Bat Mitzvah family who rented out a cruise ship, the QEII, for the party? I was invited to that one!

If I lived in a community with lavish theme Bar and Bat Mitzvah parties that diminish the sanctity of the occasion, and the celebrant did not continue their Jewish education, I would argue for the abolition of Bar and Bat Mitzvah. I would dismiss the Bar or Bat Mitzvah as a sham.

Second, I would argue that the Bar/Bat Mitzvah comes exactly at the perfect age. True, thirteen-year-olds are not really adults. Becoming an adult is a process. It does not end at thirteen, but it may well begin at about that time. How appropriate to have a Jewish ritual to mark the onset of early adulthood, the time at which young people begin to assume greater responsibilities and make more decisions for themselves. The Bar/Bat Mitzvah teaches them that Judaism expects them to study, and to consider God's will when they make their own choices.

Finally, one reason that the Bar/Bat Mitzvah is so wonderful is because it is for the individual thirteen-year-old. Being a teenager is tough. One is neither a child nor an adult. Teenagers often feel assaulted by pressures that hit them from various directions. They often seek attention, sometimes in negative ways. Jewish kids who become B'nai Mitzvah have a wonderful opportunity to have a great personal success, just when the world seems to be getting them down. How blessed we are that our Bar/Bat Mitzvah program here at Temple Beth-El assures that each one of them does have a tremendous success. How blessed is each Bat Mitzvah girl and each Bar Mitzvah boy, by his or her positive moment in the spotlight, here in the presence of God and the Jewish community.

As I began with a story from a Bar Mitzvah in Illinois, I conclude with another story, this from a Temple Beth-El Bar Mitzvah just last month. There were no bright red yarmulkes or ten-foot centerpieces. On Saturday afternoon, as I was leaving the Temple, the Bar Mitzvah boy's father told me how much the service, as well as the study which had led up to it, had meant to his son and the entire family. It was that simple.

May each of our Bar and Bat Mitzvah celebrants delight in their acquisition of Hebrew learning, draw strength as they begin to be young Jewish adults, and experience great Jewish successes. And may we continue to see them studying and practicing Judaism the week after, and for all the weeks and years of their lives. Amen.[1]

Rabbi Block truly understands the essence of the Bar Mitzvah as a "rite of passage" ceremony, celebrating the young person's first steps into adulthood. If I were sitting in the midst of his congregation during that message, I would have had to control myself from not jumping up and yelling AMEN throughout, and giving him a standing ovation at the end.

It is what Rabbi Block says so eloquently in this message that shows the heart of what I am trying to impart into the understanding of pastors, parents and youth in the Christian church around the world. Rabbi Block truly speaks the depths of my heart as he so clearly explains the true purpose of this event.

> *"May each of our Bar and Bat Mitzvah celebrants delight in their acquisition of Hebrew learning, draw strength as they begin to be young Jewish adults, and experience great Jewish successes. And may we continue to see them studying and practicing Judaism the week after, and for all the weeks and years of their lives. Amen.*

To paraphrase Rabbi Block from a Christian perspective, isn't this the desire, prayer, and goal of each Christian parent?

> *"May each of our **children Stepping Into Adulthood** delight in their acquisition of **Christian/Judaic** learning, draw strength as they begin to be young **Christian** adults, and experience great **Christian** successes. And may we continue to see them studying and practicing **Christianity** the week after, and for all the weeks and years of their lives. Amen.*

So what do you do at a "rite of passage" party? CELEBRATE! I must say that my people know how to throw a party. At Lance's Bar Mitzvah party we mixed some old with some new. We had traditional Jewish delicacies catered from a local Deli, as well as other various foods. We had one of Lance's favorite local singers sing his favorite song (theme from *The Chariots of Fire*). We even had a local group called the HaVarim Dancers. They did traditional Hebrew Folk Dances. We did the traditional lifting of the celebrant on a chair and marched him around the room. We had a wonderful time as we celebrated the words that Lance had spoken in the church service the day before. During that time, Lance spoke some Hebrew prayers that we learned together and shared publicly his love for the Lord and his desire to continue growing in that love and relationship. They were words truly worthy of a parent wanting to celebrate! Of course, Lance also received both his father's and mother's blessing, and his sister, Jeni, shared some words too.

It was a true family celebration!

One of the highlights at a traditional Bar-Mitzvah is the lighting of the candles. Each candle is lit by someone who is special to the child and/or the family. It is usually a very touching time, as a sentence or two about who the person is in relation to the celebrant is spoken as they're introduced.

Another tradition is the giving of *"gelt."* Gelt is the Yiddish word for money. It's a nice way to begin a college fund (maybe that's why there's so many Jewish doctors, lawyers and CPAs.) It can also be used as a fund to get the person's savings going for future marriage.

Whether you invite family and friends to your home for cake and ice-cream; have a potluck dinner at the church; rent a room at the local pizza parlor; rent a hall with a caterer, photographer, flowers, and the whole enchilada; or lease a jet and fly everyone to Israel to have the ceremony and celebration at the Western Wall in Jerusalem (someone actually did that) does not matter. What matters more than anything when planning this celebration is to understand what you are celebrating and why. When people who come to this celebration leave, they should take at least three things with them.

1. They should have a greater understanding of the life goals and dreams of your child, with an attitude of encouraging your child to reach for those goals.

2. They should have a greater awareness of what a "rite of passage" ceremony and celebration is.

3. They should carry with them pleasant memories of a time of tremendous blessing.

Before you go to sleep after an event like this, sit down and write me a letter. When a child takes this momentous step into adulthood, it is a very personal and meaningful event and stirs deep feelings. Let me know how everything turned out. If you're too tired after all the tumult, trust me, I'll understand. You can wait until morning.

As we say after any Jewish celebration—**Mazel Tov!**

Endnotes

During the course of my research, I spent thousands of hours on the Internet. Some of the following references were taken directly from the Internet. I have included the URL's whenever possible. Please note that the Internet is ever-changing and as a result, some of these URL's may no longer be available. I have tried whenever possible to give credit to the author's and/or writer's of any articles or material I found.

Chapter Four
1. Winkie Pratney; *Devil Take the Youngest.* (Shreveport, LA,: Huntington House, Inc., 1986).

Chapter Five
1. Craig S. Hill, *The Ancient Paths*, (Littleton, CO: Harvest Books and Publishing, 1992).
2. This is based on a study done by the Medical University of South Carolina. Found on the Internet at the following URL: http://www.musc.edu/muscid/hewchapter10.html
3. These quotes come from a number of various sources including many personal interviews. Some of the sources are also from Internet pages devoted to suicide prevention as well as the personal pages of teenagers.

Chapter Six
1. Anita Brown *The Digital Missourian* (October 27, 1995).
2. *Dallas/Fort-Worth Heritage* (March 1996). http://www.fni.com/heritage/mar96/Simba.html
3. John Marshall, *A Rite of Passage* Video from the San (Ju/Wasi) Series. You can buy or rent this video by calling Documentary Educational Resources, Inc. at 800-569-6621 or write them at D.E.R., Inc. 101 Morse St. Watertown, MA 02172
4. Peter Wallis, "Quest For The Burning Feather - Initiation For Adolescent Males." *M.E.N.* magazine (March 1996).
5. Marshall, *A Rite of Passage* Video.

Chapter Nine

1. Gary Smalley and John Trent, *The Blessing* (Nashville, TN: Thomas Nelson Publishers 1987).

Chapter Ten

1. Rabbi Barry Block's sermon was delivered at the Temple Beth-El, San Antonio, Texas, May 24, 1996. Found on the Internet: http://netxpress.com/users/beth-el/be_s0524.htm.

Bibliography, Resources and Recommended Reading

Anderson, Neil T., and Dave Park, *Stomping Out The Darkness* (Ventura, CA: Regal Books, 1993).

Bezilla, Robert, Editor, The George H. Gallup International Institute, *America's Youth In The 1990s* (Princeton, NJ, 1993).

Bly, Robert, *Iron John* (Addison/Wesley, 1990).

Capehart, Judy, *Cherishing and Challenging Your Children,* (Victor Books, 1991).

Ketterman M.D., Grace H. *You and Your Child's Problems: How To Understand and Solve Them,* (Old Tappan, NJ: Fleming H. Revell Company, 1983).

Ketterman M.D., Grace H., *A Circle of Love* (Old Tappan, NJ: Fleming H. Revell Company, 1987).

Lee, Steve, and Chap Clark, *Boys To Men* (Chicago, IL: Moody Press, 1995).

Ligon, William T., *Imparting The Blessing To Your Children,* (Brunswick, GA: Shalom, Inc., 1989).

Liptak, Karen, *Coming of Age: Traditions and Rituals Around The World* (Brookfield, CT: The Millbrook Press, 1994).

Luce, Ron, *Inspire The Fire*, Lake Mary, FL: Creation House, 1994).

McGee, Robert S., *The Search For Significance* (Houston, TX: Rapha Publishing, 1990 Second Edition).

Neff, Miriam, *Helping Teens In Crisis,* (Wheaton, IL: Tyndale House, 1993).

Oster, Merrill J., *Becoming A Man of Honor* (San Bernardino, CA: Here's Life Publishers, 1988).

Oster, Merrill J., *Becoming A Woman of Purpose* (San Bernardino, CA: Here's Life Publishers, 1989).

Poure, Ken, *Parents: Give Your Kid A Chance,* (Fresno, CA).

Pratney, Winkie, *Youth Aflame; A Manual For Discipleship,* (Minneapolis, MN: Bethany House Publishers, 1983).

Pratney, Winkie, *Devil Take the Youngest.* (Shreveport, LA,: Huntington House, Inc., 1986).

Smalley, Gary, and John Trent, Ph.D., *The Blessing*, (Nashville, TN: Thomas Nelson Publishers, 1987).

Stanley, Charles F., *A Man's Touch*, (Victor Books, 1979).

Weber, Stu, *Tender Warrior* (Multnomah Books, 1993).

Williams, Charles, *Forever A Father Always A Son*, (Victor Books, 1991).

Wilkerson, Rich, *Hold Me While You Let Me Go*, (Eugene, OR: Harvest House Publishers, 1983).

Wright, H. Norman, *The Power Of A Parents Words*, (Ventura, CA: Regal Books, 1991).

Yorkey, Mike, General Editor, *Growing A Healthy Home*, (Brentwood, TN: Wolgemuth & Hyatt, Publishers, 1990).

International Suicide/Help Lines

Lifeline: (Australia) The phone number 13 1114 allows a caller to be connected to their nearest centre from anywhere in Australia for the cost of a local call.

Kids Help Line: From anywhere in Australia, call 24 HOURS TOLL FREE on 1-800-55-1800

The Samaritans can be called at any time of the day or night. From anywhere in the UK dial 0345 90 90 90, for the cost of a local call. In the Republic of Ireland dial 1850 60 90 90, for the cost of a local call

The Suicide Information and Education Centre has a database listing just about every Crisis Intervention Center in America (listed by state) and Canada (listed by Province). You can find it on the Internet at: http://www.siec.ca/crisis.html

If you are not connected to the Internet and would like information for your state or country you can contact us at the Joy International office.

Here is a listing by country of various phone numbers of Befrienders International offices located around the world. This is the largest organization for suicide prevention

ARGENTINA	[54] 930 430
ARMENIA	[374] 2 538 194
AUSTRIA	[43] 222 713 3374
BARBADOS	[1] 809 429 9999
BRAZIL	
Sao Paulo	[55] 11 825 4111
Brasilia	[55] 61 274 4111
Centro Rio	[55] 21 233 9191

CYPRUS   [357] 220 277
DENMARK   [45] 70 201 201
EGYPT   [20] 2 344 8200
ESTONIA   [3722] 556 574
FRANCE   [3301] 45 39 93 74
HONG KONG   [852] 2 382 0000
HUNGARY   [36] 46 323 888
INDIA
  Bombay   [91] 22 307 3451
  Hyderabad   [91] 40 235 538
  Madras   [91] 44 827 3456
  New Delhi   [91] 11 371 0763
ITALY   [39] 6 7045 4444/5
JAPAN   [81] 6 251 4343
LITHUANIA   [370] 2 62 69 62
MALAYSIA   [60] 4 281 5161
NEW ZEALAND   [64] 3 366 6676
POLAND   [48] 89 52 70000
PORTUGAL   [351] 39 7210101
RUSSIA   [7] 095 152 0251
SINGAPORE   [65] 221 4444
SOUTH AFRICA   [27] 051 448 3000
SOUTH KOREA   [82] 2 715 8600
SRI LANKA   [94] 1 692 909
SWEDEN   [46] 31 711 2400
THAILAND   [66] 2 2499977
TRINIDAD   [1] 809 645 2800
YUGOSLAVIA   [381] 21 623 393
ZIMBABWE   [263] 4 722000

ABOUT THE AUTHOR

Jeff Brodsky is a Messianic Jew who was born and raised in Brooklyn, New York. Jeff accepted Jesus as his Messiah in October of 1974. He has been in full-time ministry to children, youth and families for the past eighteen years. He is president and founder of Joy International (begun in 1981), and has traveled to more than forty countries.

Jeff has a unique style of ministry and is recognized as a master storyteller. He has spoken and ministered in Churches, Schools, Seminaries, Conferences, Seminars, and the streets around the world. Jeff has a marvelous ability to keep the attention of both adults as well as children with his insight and humor.

He loves children and committed his life to serving the Lord by serving them. This is currently accomplished through his ministry to parents in his "Step Into Adulthood" Seminars.

Jeff and his wife Gail have three children - Brent (25), Jeni (21) and Lance (19). When not traveling, Jeff ministers to children and families at Faith Ministries Christian Outreach Centre in Denver, Colorado as well as serving as President of Joy International.

JOY INTERNATIONAL

Joy International is an organization founded by Jeff Brodsky in July of 1981. The following are all ministries of Joy International:

STEP INTO ADULTHOOD SEMINARS

This seminar is changing lives all over the world. A seven hour seminar that covers all the material in this book. Jeff has been invited to do these Seminars throughout the world. At this writing he has received invitations from eighteen countries.

JOY INTERNATIONAL CHILDREN'S HOMES AND ADOPTIONS

Joy International currently sponsors children's homes in India, and has homes under construction in Venezuela and Fiji. This area of their ministry is growing rapidly as they are now in the process of establishing the Joy International Adoption Agency.

ANNUAL 101 MILE DEATH VALLEY WALK

This walk has grown from the original five walkers the first year, to nearly one hundred this coming year. It includes youth and families from all over the world. Each walker gets sponsors per mile. The funds raised, go towards the expenses of the Joy International Children's Homes as well as the expenses of International Adoptions.

CHILDREN'S AND YOUTH WORKERS SEMINARS

After working with children for nearly seventeen years both as an international evangelist and on the local church level, Jeff has so much to share. His Children's and Youth Workers Seminars will help to motivate, train and inspire the workers in your church from Nursery help to Children's Church through High School.

For more information on how you can:
- Schedule a Step Into Adulthood Seminar
- Participate in the next Annual 101 Mile Death Valley Walk
- Schedule a Children's Worker's Seminar
- Get additional information about the Joy International Children's Homes and International Adoptions
- Order additional copies of this book

Or if you need any other information regarding any of the ministries of Joy International, you can contact us at any of the following:

Joy International
P.O. Box 5399
Englewood, CO 80155 - USA

Nationwide Toll Free: **1-888-JOY-4-ALL (569-4255)**
Phone: **303-766-2650**
Fax: **303-766-3303**
E-Mail: **jeff@joy.org**

Please visit our Website on the Internet at:
http://www.joy.org